The Basques

A Captivating Guide to the History of the Basque Country, Starting from Prehistory through Roman Rule and the Middle Ages to the Present

Free Bonus from Captivating History
(Available for a Limited time)

Hi History Lovers!

Now you have a chance to join our exclusive history list so you can get your first history ebook for free as well as discounts and a potential to get more history books for free! Simply visit the link below to join.

Captivatinghistory.com/ebook

Also, make sure to follow us on Facebook, Twitter and Youtube by searching for Captivating History.

Contents

Introduction

The Basques live in a portion of the Pyrenees in the far southwestern corner of France and across the ridge in the north-central portion of Spain, centered on the towns of Pamplona and Donostia. While some live outside this area today, many still call this region home. These hardy people have dwelt in the foothills of the jagged Pyrenees Mountains since prehistoric times, and they're still there to this day.

The Basques manifest a genetic makeup that is prehistorically distinct from that of their neighbors in Spain or France. This has puzzled scientists and researchers for years. A genetic study conducted by Uppsala University in Sweden in 2015 discovered that the Basques established themselves as an ethnic group during Neolithic times, anywhere from 12,000 to 4,500 years ago.

The Basques were isolated from other human migrations into Europe for millennia. Anthropologists have said that they are descendants of the Neolithic farmers who intermingled with a hunter-gatherer culture. About 850,000 pure Basques live in Spain, while 130,000 dwell in France.

Their language is unique; it is a "language isolate," meaning it has no genealogical relationship with other languages. It is not one of the "Romance" languages, that is, derived from Latin. It is not derived from the Indo-European family of languages either, which is characteristic of Germany, Europe, or the Slavic countries.

The principal propelling agent for the success of the Basques throughout the ages is the people's need for survival. For generations, the Basques lived in the foothills and mountains of the Pyrenees. They learned how to harness that challenging terrain and make it their own.

In Spain, the Basques mainly live in the Southern Basque Country, which is composed of three provinces. Álava (or Araba-Álava), Biscay (or Vizcaya), and Gipuzkoa are autonomous Spanish Basque communities, which means they have their own administration and political organizations, as well as their own leaders, legislatures, courts, and assemblies. Navarre is also an autonomous community, but it has separated itself from the other three provinces. They continue to have a relationship with the country of Spain in terms of taxation and tariffs.

In France, many Basques live in the Northern Basque Country, also called the French Basque Country. It lays west of the Pyrénées-Atlantique. The Northern Basque Country incorporates the three historical Basque provinces of Labourd, Soule, and Lower Navarre. In 2017, a single commonwealth was created in France for the French Basque Country, and it is known as the Agglomerate Community of Basque Country. The French Basque Country is also called *Iparralde*. In Basque, it means the "northern region."

There is also a diaspora of Basque, who mostly live in France, Spain, the United States South America, and a curious collection of French islands called Saint Pierre and Miquelon.

A great effort has been made here to present the clearest explanation possible to elucidate the history of these fascinating people. However, through the ravages of history and its turnover of conquerors, the borders of the Basque lands have shifted, and the names of places have changed with unnerving frequency.

Chapter 1 – The Mystery of the Mountain People

The Basque Country

The greater Basque Country, also known as *Euskal Herria* (the oldest documented name for the home of the Basques), is located in the northeastern corner of Spain and southwestern France. The region is about three million square miles, and it is home to around three million inhabitants. It is a mountainous country in the Pyrenees, but the heights of the jagged mountain peaks do not exceed 3,500 feet. In the winter, the mountaintops are covered with snow. The terrain slopes down into the fertile valley of the Ebro River.

The Basques have beaches made of either sand or rocks. The mountains have many caverns, some of which contain paintings of bears rendered by early man. There are forests in this region as well, and the southern region of the Basque Country even has a desert. The weather is cool and damp in the north, as it lies on the coast of the northern Atlantic.

Today, the Basque Country is known as the cultural region of the Basques, and it is split into three areas: the Basque Autonomous Community in Spain, the Chartered Community of Navarre, and *Iparralde*, or the French Basque Country. The northern provinces border the Bay of Biscay. "Bisc" and its variation of "Visc" stands for Vascones (or Viscones), the largest historical tribe of the Basques.

The Basque cultural region consists of provinces that have large numbers of Basques living among people from other cultures, mainly those of French and Spanish backgrounds. Those provinces are Labourd (*Lapurdi*), Lower Navarre (*Nafarroa Beherea*), and Soule (*Zuberoa*). The most common language of the Basque Autonomous Community is *Euskara*. Others outside of the region simply call it the Basque language. The cultural region also has some who speak French or Spanish, in addition to speaking Basque.

Mysterious Origins

Archaeological investigations seem to indicate the earliest hominids arrived in the Basque Country during the Paleolithic era, more specifically between 43,000 and 23,000 years ago, possibly even earlier. The Paleolithic era, also known as the Old Stone Age, refers to the first prehistorical period in which humans developed stone tools. It coincides with what is called the Pleistocene, or the Ice Age, at which time the glaciers started to recede.

It appears that humans migrated from Eastern Europe to Western Europe and eventually to the Basque Country. Their culture was called the Aurignacian. The skeletal remains of *Homo antecessor* and *Homo heidelbergensis*, along with primitive tools, were found in a cave called the El Portalón in Atapuerca, Spain. *Homo heidelbergensis* is the oldest human fossil in the world. Some believe that *Homo neanderthalensis* ("Neanderthals") descended from *Homo heidelbergensis*. However, the existence of *Homo heidelbergensis* as a separate species is highly debatable. Relationships between these archaic, now extinct species are unclear, but they were ancestors of *Homo sapiens*, which are modern humans.

In the Cantabrian region, which lies just west of the current-day Basque Country, rock art was discovered in a cave in Aitzbitarte Hill, dating back to the Paleolithic era. In the Isturitz and Oxocelhaya caverns in the Basque Country, located in the province of Navarre, human bones were also found, specifically cranial vaults used as drinking vessels, bone flutes, and cave paintings of lion cubs and oxen. Navarre in is the Pyrenees, near the French border.

The Santimamiñe Cave in the Basque Country displays cave art of not only bison, wooly mammoths, wooly rhinoceroses, horses, and bears—it also shows pictures of lions. Fossil remains of lions dating back from 191,000 to 11,700 years ago were actually found in Europe from the Pleistocene period. In fact, this cave contains the complete skeleton of a lion. Lions and rhinoceroses have never been seen in the wilds of Western Europe during recorded history, especially in the colder mountain regions. However, it is quite possible that the ancient Basques hunted lions. The Santimamiñe Cave, where those fossils were found, is near the coast of the Bay of Biscay, west of the French border in the Pyrenees.

In the Gatzarria Cave in the French Pyrenees, which lies east of the Basque Country, there are remnants of the carcasses of red deer and bison. There is evidence of the existence of Neanderthals at this site, but the general consensus is that the human population there was less dense.

Differences between the Iberians and the Basques

As indicated in the studies reported in the Proceedings of the National Academy of Sciences of the United States of America, Torsten Gunther and other researchers of Uppsala University in Sweden discovered that ancient Iberian farmers mixed with the "hunter-gatherers" who were already in the Basque Country between 25 million to 12,000 years ago during the Paleolithic era. Iberians were the ancient people who lived in today's countries of Spain and Portugal—the Iberian Peninsula, in other words.

The origin of the Basques is controversial to this day. Language is frequently used as a tool by anthropologists to discover the origin of a society. However, linguists have already seen differences between the Basque language and the Iberian language. In addition, they also have discovered that the Basque language differs from other Indo-

European languages. Linguistic analyses conclude that the Basque language may be related to that of the hunter-gatherers who preceded the agriculturally-oriented Basques, who came in during the Neolithic times. Their language is truly unique. Because efforts to find similarities in the Basque language and the ancient Iberian language have failed, the two groups were initially distinct from one another when the Basques settled the land. The Basque language, or *Euskara* as the Basques call it, is a language isolate, which is a unique language that is very unlike the languages spoken in neighboring lands. In order to determine the origin of an ethnic group, scientists use not only genetic factors but also language. Members of the same tribe often speak the same tongue, and that generally continues to be spoken throughout the generations. As they mix and mingle with other tribes over time, though, new words and new pronunciations infiltrate.

However, there is still an unanswered question. Who were the hunter-gatherers who spoke the Basque language and preceded the Iberian farmer migrants into the Basque Country?

DNA studies conducted by the Genographic Project for the National Geographic Society have shown that the genetic structure of the Basque people is different from that of the Iberians. Also, ancient Iberians populated Spain abound 7,000 years ago, placing them in the Mesolithic/Neolithic era (the Middle/Late Stone Age). The Basques, however, appear to have originated in the Paleolithic era, thus predating the Iberians. Those who were called "Iberians" arrived after the Basques. In fact, the DNA studies on the Basques show they are *not* of Indo-European origin, while the Iberians are.

Geneticists have analyzed Basque mitochondrial DNA and discovered that there are similar chromosomal markers and other DNA evidence from people from the Ural Mountains of Russia. They are attempting to discover if there is a relationship between the two, but evidence for that determination is unclear at the moment.

To sum up, the origin of the Basques is an enigma, and only time will tell if more information arises to help dispel the mists surrounding their murky beginnings.

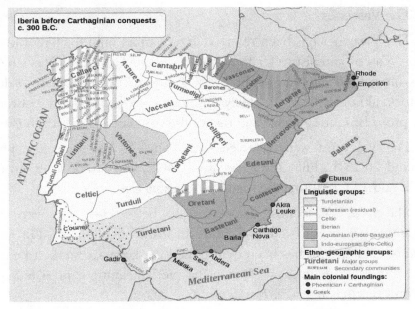

Basque tribes in the Iberian Peninsula

The Basque Tribes

The early tribes of the Basques were known as the Vascones, the Autrigones, the Caristii, the Varduli, the Vescetani, the Iacentani, the Tarbelli, the Suburates, the Biguerres, and the Aquitanians. Territories occupied by the Tarbelli, the Suburates, the Biguerres, and the Aquitanians lay within the southwestern portion of current-day France. In his book, *Commentaries on the Gallic Wars* (published between 58 and 49 BCE), Julius Caesar noted that their land "looks between the setting sun and the North Star." Although Caesar noted them in his book, he was far from the first to talk about them. The earliest written history of that area coincided with the arrival of the Roman Empire in 196 BCE, prior to Caesar's reign.

Through history, the term "Vascones" has come to be associated with the Basques, but there is no evidence that the Vascones were the ancestors of today's Basques. Some of the ancient tombstones from the Roman era bear names of Vascones, so that is just one of the terms the Romans applied to them.

The Vascones

The Vascones has been referred to as a tribe, but the etymological root "Vasco" can also refer to all the Basques. The word "Vascones" was often used interchangeably with "Basques" throughout recorded history, although linguistic analyses show a strong similarity between the proto-Basque language and that of the Aquitanians, a French tribe.

The Vascones were referred to by ancient historians like Livy around 76 BCE, Pliny the Elder in 50 BCE, and Strabo between 63 BCE and 14 CE during the reign of Augustus Caesar.

The term "Vascones" also came to be synonymous with the Basques because of cultural and linguistic similarities. Through linguistic analysis, it has been determined the language spoken by the prehistorical Vascones was "proto-Basque," meaning it predated the current Basque language, *Euskara*.

When the Romans came raging in, the Vascones reached an agreement with Julius Caesar by granting Rome access to Iberia, allowing the Romans to go from Gaul (France), over the Pyrenees, and through their territory. As part of their agreement, the Vascones weren't subjected to heavy colonization by the Romans during the Roman Republic. Instead, they were recruited by the ancient Romans as mercenary soldiers.

The Aquitanians

Aquitania was a tribal nation consisting of a number of sub-tribes. The western portion of Aquitania became part of the Basque Country. When the earliest people inhabited this land, they were hunters. Archaeological evidence of Aquitanian art shows figures of extinct animals such as the wooly mammoth and the tarpan. The tarpan was a wild horse that was smaller than today's horse. Besides these extinct species, the Aquitanians hunted bison, deer, and goats.

They had oxen and boars, and they were one of the earliest people to domesticate the dog.

Although prehistoric Aquitanians did become farmers, agriculture arrived very late, and it wasn't widespread until later. It may have occurred toward the end of the Neolithic period during the New Stone Age some 12,000 years ago. Some historians, though, contradict that opinion based on genetic evidence. They believe that it coincided with the Early Iron Age instead. Today, agriculture is the secondary occupation of these hardy people. Technology is their primary occupation now.

Julius Caesar describes the Aquitanian tribe in his famed book, *Commentaries on the Gallic Wars*. One of the most-quoted lines in his book is about the Aquitanians: "All Gaul is divided into three parts, one of which the Belgae inhabit, and the Aquitani another." The Belgae were a collection of tribes living in Gaul. Aquitania was in southwestern "Celtica," the early Roman word for France. The Aquitanians were sometimes called "Gallia Belgica," meaning "long-haired Gaul." Caesar divided the Aquitanian land into "Aquitania Prima" in the northeast, "Aquitania Secunda" in the central region, and "Aquitania Tertia" in the southwest.

During their campaign to conquer the Iberian Peninsula, the Romans fought many battles against the Aquitanian tribe. However, they did occupy some areas there and set up settlements. The Basque tribes realized they wouldn't be subject to Roman law, and they were able to keep their culture and customs intact.

The Autrigones

Strabo called the Autrigones the "Allótrigones," a word that means "strange people." He also added that "the rough and savage manners of these people is not alone owing to their wars, but likewise to their isolated position." Strabo was referring to the 4th century BCE when the Autrigones overran Cantabria and Burgos, which were territories just to their west.

The Caristii and Varduli Tribes

The Caristii occupied an area along the coast of the Bay of Biscay off the northern coast of Spain. The Santimamiñe Cave is located there. There is no indication of any resistance to the Roman occupation by these two tribes. In fact, the Varduli served as mercenaries during the Roman period. They even assisted the Romans in the conquest of Britannia.

The Iacentani

The Iacentani people were a sub-tribe of the Aquitanians. In 195 BCE, they were overwhelmed by the Vescetani people (see below), who devastated and sacked their towns and lands. The Iacentani lands were then annexed and made part of the territory of the Vescetani.

The Vescetani

These people could have been the Aquitanian tribe that dwelled on the northern tributary of the Ebro River. The Vescetani may have been part of the Celtic migration into the northern Pyrenees territory around 600 BCE. The Vescetani cooperated with the Roman conquest but later rebelled. Under Commander Gaius Terentius Varro, they were vanquished, and the Romans took over their territory.

They may have been assimilated into the territory of the Vascones by the 2nd century BCE because their names do not appear in the ancient texts of Ptolemy or Strabo.

The Tarbelli

The Tarbelli dwelled in today's province of Labourd in the French Basque Country. Linguists have identified their dialect as being related to that of the Aquitanians. Julius Caesar called them the "Tarbelli of the four banners," meaning they consisted of four subtribes.

The Suburates

Ancient history indicates that this tribe inhabited the current-day province of Soule in the French Basque Country. Like the Tarbelli, they were related to the Aquitanians. Julius Caesar also mentions them as having surrendered some hostages as a token of submission to the conquering Romans.

The Biguerres

The Biguerres were one of the Aquitanian tribes that surrendered to Marcus Licinius Crassus, Caesar's lieutenant. The origin of the term "Biguerres" might have come from the word "ibai gorri," which means "red river." It could have been referring to the Garonne River that runs through Aquitaine, as that river has a distinctive brownish-red tinge.

Neighboring Tribes

The Cantabrians

During the Bronze Age, around the year 2500 BCE, some Celts came to the Basque Country. Some of them settled in the western Iberian Peninsula, but others migrated northeast to the coast. Some intermarried with the indigenous Basques.

According to Roman Senator Cato the Elder, the main river of Cantabria was the Ebro River, which runs through the Pyrenees. He stated, "The Ebro River starts in the land of Cantabri, large and beautiful, with abundant fish."

The Cantabrians spoke a very early form of the Celtic language as opposed to *Euskara*, the language of the Basques. Although the Cantabrians were once considered to be one of the early Basque tribes, it is now known that their origin isn't Basque; it is Celtic. In Roman times, the Cantabrians inhabited an area just west of the Basque regions.

The Astures

The Astures dwelled west of Cantabria, along the coast of the Bay of Biscay. They were matrilineal, which means women were considered to be the heads of the household. They inherited money and even fought in wars alongside men.

Chapter 2 – The Ancient Mystery Unravels

Basques in the Chalcolithic Era

"Chalcolithic" is the term applied to the Copper Age, which was the era just preceding the Bronze Age. The earliest artifacts from the Chalcolithic Age in the Basque Country have been dated to around 2500 BCE.

The people sought to develop tools more malleable than stone. Copper was mined in the Basque region, which can be melted so that it is soft enough to hammer into tools. Once it is mixed with tin, it becomes bronze.

The Basques created "bell beakers," as did other Iberian peoples. Bell beakers were common in the Western Pyrenees, which includes the Basque territory. The bell beaker, which was made from terracotta clay, was shaped like a wide vase. Some of those bell beakers were used to heat up fresh copper. The bell beakers were also used as drinking vessels—although they were rather large ones—from which the Basques drank mead, a fermented honey wine. The bell beakers were also used to hold grain or other foods and drinks. The pottery during this time was undecorated.

The Basques in the Bronze Age

The Bronze Age covered the period of 1700 to 700 BCE. Bronze wasn't as plentiful in the Basque territory, and it was mostly used for practical uses, such as cooking pots, or in fortifications and ornamentation. The Basques had a prolonged Bronze Age in comparison to the surrounding areas. This was due to their isolation.

The pottery made by the Basques during the Bronze Age became more highly decorated. A lot of it was "corded," meaning the creator would make ropes out of plant fibers and twist them up into a cord. The cords would be wrapped around the vessel. After they were removed, a decorative impression was left behind. They are sometimes called "cordons."

Bronze tools and weapons were also made, including axes, spears, and arrowheads.

Basque Burial Customs

To commemorate their dead, the prehistorical Basques built dolmens, which are monuments consisting of two immense vertical stones supporting a horizontal stone. These were mostly made of limestone, which was the most common stone in the Basque Country. Most Basque graves were common graves, but some had chambers. As one might expect, people from the higher classes were buried in the graves with more than one chamber. By the Iron Age, bodies were cremated.

It was important that the burials be made close to the villages that the people once inhabited. Some families even buried their loved ones beneath their homes.

In later years, after the Basques were Christianized, they were buried near the churches they attended. Crosses were carved on their tombstones. Bells sounded for funerals, and the knelling was different for men than for women. The mourners were expected to make donations to the grieving family, especially if the deceased had very young children. At weddings, it was customary for the bride and groom to visit the gravesites of their close relatives. It was a way in which the family was "introduced" to the new couple. The bride would bring candles and flowers to symbolize respect and love for those who had died.

When the family visited the graves of loved ones, they might leave a piece of wood carved in the shape of a person and coated with wax.

The Basques in the Iron Age

The Iron Age, which followed the Bronze Age, arrived in the Basque Country around 600 BCE. Burial customs changed during that timeframe. Instead of collective burials in mounds, bodies were cremated and then buried inside stone circles called cromlechs.

During the Iron Age, the Basques became more agricultural. Cereal crops, like millet, wheat, and quinoa, were grown.

Basque Mythology and Religion

Each village had its own gods and goddesses. One of the more popular goddesses was Mari, the main goddess of the Basque religion. She was the "earth mother." Mari was symbolized by a round disk called the *luburu*. When the great goddess was in her underground dwelling, she was displayed in an animal form, which was either a horse, goat, or vulture. The Basques lived in the mountains, and they saw caves as safe places to dwell.

When she was displayed during the day, Mari was depicted as a long-haired, beautiful woman in a red tunic with a dragon at her feet. Mari held a golden crown in her right hand. Her consort was Sugaar, and Mari occasionally would join Sugaar to create storms. These storms were beneficial to the people because they brought much-needed rain for their crops, although sometimes they were destructive. Sugaar was sometimes represented as a male serpent. Mari and Sugaar had two sons: Atarrabi (or Atxular), who represents good, and Mikelats, who represents evil.

The Basque creation story is very similar to those told by other cultures around the world. In the beginning, there was nothing but darkness. Then Mari gave birth to a daughter, Ilargi, the moon. When Mari's people complained that the moon did not give sufficient light, Mari gave birth to another daughter, who was Eguzki, the sun.

At night, the terrors that haunt the land were sometimes extreme, so Mari gave her people the flower of the sun, which was known as the Eguzkilore. It was a flower that resembled a thistle. She advised her people to display this flower on their doors to protect them from the specters of the night.

The Basques followed a Chthonic cult. It promoted the belief in an underworld. The underworld they ascribed to wasn't necessarily beneath the earth per se; it was more like a place for the undercurrent of deities, which influenced people and events. The Basques cherished many legends, some of which contained beings called *mairuak*, who were the giant builders of their grave monuments, cromlechs, and stone circles. The *jentilak* was a race of powerful giants who built megalithic monuments. The *iratxoak* were imps, the *sorginak* referred to witches and priestesses, and the *basajaunak* were the wild men and women of the woods.

During medieval times, a local Basque legend relates that the Basques were descendants of Tubal, the grandson of Noah. Tubal was one of the sons of Japheth. Japheth and Tubal came from an ancient biblical tribe that departed Mesopotamia and settled in Iberia along the Ebro River.

Over the years, even during the prehistorical era, tales about the gods and goddesses have changed. In the town of Biarritz, in Labourd province, for example, the people taught that Mari did not dwell in the cave; she dwelt on the highest mountains. That legend instructs the people that Mari divided the people into two groups: the people who lived during the day—the *egunekoak*—and the people who lived at night—the *gauekoak*. The people weren't always seen as human; they were disembodied beings or spirits of the dead.

Death in the Basque Mythology

First of all, the Basques focused on the importance of a "good death." According to a prominent Basque anthropologist, Annuntxi Arana, oral stories were passed on from generation to generation, and they highlighted the fact that a "good death" implied that the person lived a good life. Prayers on behalf of the dying person were essential to keeping the evil spirits at bay. A "bad death," meaning a violent death, was the work of magical intervention. Another sign of a bad or troubled death was the weather close to the time of one's passing.

People often used amulets to protect themselves from the evil spirits that were attracted to those who were dying.

Mythical entities called *lamiak* were good spirits who dwelled near waterways. They were the opposite of the mythological sirens from Greek mythology, who allowed men's ships to crash on the rocky shore. Instead, the *lamiak* would aid people when they were in need as long as the supplicants left gifts. *Lamiak* were believed to help in the birth of a child. They were also summoned when someone was about to die so they could help aid them. They were, in essence, "good witches."

Kind women existed outside of myths as well. At times, women provided herbal remedies to ease the pain of suffering. They rendered their services not only for those who were dying but also for those who simply needed some kind of treatment.

The early Basques believed specters and symbols of death would visit people to alert them to an impending death, whether it was their own death or that of someone close to them. Some typical death omens were a cock crowing during the night or the incessant barking of dogs.

In some interpretations, the Basque goddess Mari dwelled in the world of the dead—a cave, if you will. She symbolized the passage of a person moving from the land of the living into the underworld. It should be noted the Basque underworld was not seen as a negative place like Hell. Instead, it was the cave of the spirits. The dead could be resurrected into the land of the living as a breath or a gentle wind, and they could live comfortably among the living. However, if a person left a serious matter unresolved, that might conjure up their spirit into the waking world. These visitations were sometimes accompanied by strange noises at night, and the person who was being "warned" was expected to find some way of making restitution for his or her offense.

The Afterlife

According to the Basques, when a person died, they were transformed into another mode of existence. If their life was a good one, they would go down the path into the underworld and into Mari's cave. Then they would be led to a land of peace, abundance, and overwhelming happiness. If they had committed offenses during their life, and as long as those offenses were not too numerous or severe, they were made to wander for a while in the dark, seeking Mari's cave. When they found it, they were welcomed in. However, if a person was truly evil, he or she would be forced to wander about in the darkness, harassed by evil spirits forever.

The cave utilized in the Basque mythology relates to their early prehistory, during which time they needed to take shelter from the glaciers or weather through the storms. For the prehistoric Basques, caves were safe places.

Chapter 3 – The Basques under the Roman Empire

The Basques during the Punic Wars and the Roman Conquest

In the 3rd century BCE, Carthage, a port city in North Africa, was interested in trade and wanted to expand so it could include colonies surrounding the Mediterranean. In 246 BCE, Carthage became involved in a massive conflict with Rome, which was also expanding. These clashes were known as the "Punic" Wars, after the Roman term for Carthage. There were three Punic Wars altogether.

Although the Vascones once worked for the Romans as mercenaries, during the Punic Wars, they fought on the side of the Carthaginians. Therefore, the Basque tribes weren't always mercenaries for Rome. It all depended upon the circumstances under which they were hired and the year of the engagements.

The Carthaginians annexed and colonized cities around the Mediterranean Sea and established the Carthaginian Empire. Between the years 237 and 218 BCE, the Carthaginians boldly infiltrated the Iberian Peninsula and traveled northward. Upon reaching the areas in the far north, they encountered the Basques. The Carthaginians weren't interested in settling the Basque Country, which they called "Vasconia," but they depended upon the Basques to become mercenaries to help them conquer new lands. Many able-bodied Vascones readily accepted that role and were paid in gold and silver. In 216 BCE, the Vascones marched with Hannibal across the Alps and into Italy. Hannibal, though, was unable to march on Rome itself because he lacked siege engines.

The city of Carthage itself was destroyed in 146 BCE, and once the Vascones and other Basque tribes saw that destruction, they were reluctant to go up against the Romans ever again.

The Sertorian War

The Romans brought their civil war with them when they occupied Spain. Between the years 88 and 80 BCE, two Roman consuls, Gaius Marius and Lucius Cornelius Sulla, opposed each other, as both wanted full control of the Roman territories.

Quintus Sertorius was the governor of Hispania. He was considered a moderate governor, and he treated the conquered people fairly. Because of political conflicts in Italy, Serortius became a rebellious Roman.

Sertorius supported the Marian faction, but when Sulla won the civil war and became a tyrant in Rome, Sulla sent a force to Hispania to defeat Sertorius and his supporters. Sertorius then fled to Tingis in North Africa (near Morocco). To his surprise, Sertorius was met by emissaries from the Lusitanians, a Hispanic tribe in the northwest of the peninsula. Having heard about his reputation, the Lusitanians sought to recruit him to ward off the Roman soldiers sent by Sulla. Believing that he might be able to force Rome to get rid of Sulla, Sertorius returned to Hispania and rallied a force of like-minded rebellious Romans. He met with initial success and even defeated the Roman governor of Hispania Ulterior (the Latin term for the Iberian Peninsula).

Sertorius then sent out his commander, Lucius Hirtuleius, who unseated the Sulla-appointed ruler in Hispania Citerior (the eastern coast of Iberia) and Hispania Tarraconensis (covered much of modern-day Spain). Because of the Sertorian threat, Sulla raised the status of Hispania to a proconsular province and sent over Quintus Caecilius Metellus Pius to act as a governor. Pius sent over his own commander, Domitius Calvinus, to seize Hispania Ulterior. He was blocked by fortifications built by Hirtuleius.

Hirtuleius and his men waged sporadic guerilla warfare. Little by little, the Roman forces moved inland, and Sertorius tried to fight them off. When Metellus Pius discovered this, he sent in his own armies. However, after many successful strikes by Sertorius, Metellus Pius called for reinforcements from Gallia Transalpina ("Transalpine Gaul"). They crossed the Pyrenees and waged battle with Hirtuleius but were defeated and forced to retreat to Gaul.

The Battle of Lauron

Rome then dispatched Gnaeus Pompeius Magnus, better known as Pompey, to seize control of the Spanish territories from Sertorius. In 76 BCE, Pompey marched along the Mediterranean coast of Hispania toward the town of Lauron. His troops were in need of supplies and sent out men to forage. Sertorius harassed them when they returned to join the troops, but then Sertorius sent in his heavy armored infantry divisions from the woods, which was followed by Sertorius's cavalry.

When Pompey discovered the foragers' predicament, he sent out a legion, but it was roundly defeated. Thankfully for him, he still had a sizeable force left.

Metellus Pius joined up with Pompey. They continued to work their way north through midland Hispania. Pompey then decided to circumvent the Romans and move toward northern Hispania.

The Battle of Italica

This battle, fought in 75 BCE between the forces of Hirtuleius and Metellus Pius, illustrates some of the Roman military's famous tactics. Metellus Pius attacked the weaker flanks first on either side and then encircled the Sertorian warriors in the center. It worked well, and Metellus Pius and the Romans won. Hirtuleius lost over 20,000 men.

Pamplona

In the winter of 75 CE, Pompey moved farther north of the Ebro and stopped at a town called Iruna, along the Arga River (known as the Runa River in contemporary history). He felt it was ideal for his encampment. The Arga River is a tributary of the Ebro in the modern-day Basque province of Álava. This was in the heart of the Vascone territory.

Pompey descended upon Iruna and called it "Pompaelo" (Pamplona), which is named after him. The city was in a strategic location, as it was close to the border of Gaul (France), La Rioja, and Aragon (the latter two areas are provinces of Hispania). All three of these areas were close to the Pyrenees and the border of Gaul. In ancient times, La Rioja was inhabited by the Autrigones and the Vascones. In addition, it was inhabited by the Berones, which was an ancient Celtic tribe.

When Pompey arrived, he immediately had his forces build heavy stone walls around the city. Those stone walls have been modified and rebuilt many times throughout history. The remnants of these walls still stand today. They were sometimes extended to enclose protected settlements belonging to the Romans and to other ethnic groups later on.

Fractures

Divisive elements erupted between the Iberians and the Roman Sertorian forces. The Romans were abusive of the Iberians, which, of course, kindled discontent. In fact, Sertorius himself was becoming paranoid, though that was probably for a justifiable reason. Taking advantage of the friction that had developed between the Iberians and the Roman troops under Sertorius, Metellus Pius made an offer. Any Roman who betrayed Sertorius would receive a reward of 100 silver talents and 20,000 acres of land. In 73 BCE, one of Sertorius's

Roman commanders, Marcus Perperna Vento, organized some conspirators, and they murdered Sertorius.

Perperna attempted to regain the support of the Sertorians, but Pompey laid a trap for him. Pompey used the old tactic of the feigned retreat. He gathered up ten cohorts and hastily pulled back in the midst of fighting. As soon as Perperna and his forces rushed forward to confront them, Pompey's men suddenly turned heel and surprised them. It was a massacre.

Pompey returned with a vengeance, and he eventually defeated Sertorius and his forces in southern Spain. The Vascones then returned to their native land. The ancient chronicler Livy indicates that little Romanization of the Basque territories occurred during the Roman occupation because Vasconia was so mountainous. Therefore, the Vascones and other Basque tribes were relatively free from Roman intrusion and control. Being mercenary soldiers rather than Roman subjects was to their advantage.

Roman Expansion under Crassus

In 58 BCE, the general Publius Licinius Crassus conquered some of the Aquitanian tribes to the north and east of Pamplona. Today, that Aquitanian territory is now the Basque Autonomous Community of Navarre. The Sotiates, a Gallic-Aquitani tribe, fought poorly in the battles against Crassus. This was because they left their rear weak, which resulted in a Roman victory. According to Caesar in his book, *Commentaries on the Gallic Wars*, "At last, after heavy casualties, a large number of the enemy fled from the field. A large number of them were slain."

Julius Caesar helped Crassus expand Roman territory and went up against Vercingetorix, the chieftain from the Arverni tribe of Gaul. He united a number of Gallic tribes to rebel against the Romans. His forces engaged Caesar at the Battle of Gergovia in 52 BCE. Vercingetorix won, but he was subsequently defeated by the Romans at Alesia in the same year.

It is interesting to note that Caesar made a clear distinction between the language of the Aquitanians and that of the Gauls. The Aquitanians spoke a form of "proto-Basque," the precursor of the Basque language, while the Gauls spoke a Celtic language.

The Cantabrian Wars

In 29 BCE, the Romans invaded the mountainous area inhabited by the Astures and the Cantabrians. For a portion of the wars, the Astur general was Gausón, while the Cantabrian commander was Corocotta. Cantabria was located along the northern coast of Hispania. The ancient historian Lucius Flores wrote that it was "that part which adjoins the cliffs where the Pyrenees end and is washed by the nearer waters of the ocean."

The Roman army would eventually be overseen by the emperor himself, Caesar Augustus. A victory over the Astures would shine a spotlight on Augustus's reign, as the Astures were noted for their ferocity and skill in using light armaments. This neighboring Basque tribe also used a special breed of horse called the Asturcón, named after the Astures. It is a short, stocky horse, and it was first described by the ancient historian Pliny the Elder. The horse is still bred today.

At that time, Cantabria was an independent region occupied by the Celtic Iberians (Celtiberians), and the Astures lived in a territory just to the west of them. The Astures and the Cantabrians agreed to cooperate so they could fight off the Romans. In 26 BCE, Augustus Caesar set up his encampment at Segisama (modern-day Sasamon, Spain), just to the east of Cantabria, with about 70,000 men. He split up his forces into three divisions, which the Cantabrians and Astures did as well.

The Siege of Aracillum

In 25 BCE, the Romans stormed up the Cantabrian Mountains with about 25,000 men and moved toward the town of Aracillum. The Cantabrians had an equal number of warriors. The Cantabrians had a hill fort there with about twelve miles of walls, battlements, and trenches. The Roman forces under Augustus Caesar and Gaius Antistius Vetus placed the Cantabrian fort under siege. Although the Cantabrians were able to hold up for quite some time, they eventually ran out of supplies. This was a distinct Roman victory.

The Cantabrians avoided being taken prisoner by committing suicide. In fact, this was the custom of both the Cantabrians and the Astures. They used a poison made from yew trees.

The Battle of Vellica

During the same year, the Cantabrians drew Augustus Caesar and his forces, which numbered a little over 5,000 warriors, out on the plain of Mave. Normally, when the Cantabrians had to fight in an open area, they preferred to set up their battlefield so as to situate a natural border against the enemies' backs. The Romans thought that maneuver was clever and gave it the name *circulus cantabricus,* meaning "Cantabrian circle." In the case of Vellica, it wasn't going to work.

Although they could have used their hill fortress as a base of operations, the Cantabrians didn't have enough supplies to defend the fort. It may have invited a siege they couldn't withstand. Despite the Cantabrians trying to think logically about the battle, the Romans handily won and moved westward toward the land of the Astures.

Battle near the Astura River

In the spring, three Roman legions under Augustus Caesar prepared to attack the land of the Astures. According to the ancient scholars, the Astur army descended the snow-capped mountains in droves. The first phase consisted of a series of guerilla-style attacks. The Astures then headed toward their fortified town of Lancia. Unfortunately, one division of the Astures betrayed their fellow warriors and gave Augustus Caesar an advance warning about the fortifications in Lancia.

The Romans moved upon Lancia and placed the town under siege. Although the ancient records are unclear, the Astur commander

Gausón was either captured and executed at Lancia or died there during the siege.

Battle at Mons Medullius

Following that, the Astur army took refuge at Mons Medullius. The Romans dug a huge ditch (eighteen miles long!) and a moat alongside the mountain to prevent the Astures from escaping. Once they realized they were unable to repel the Romans, the Astures began committing suicide. According to the ancient historian Florus, "The barbarians, seeing that their last hour had come, vied with one another in hastening their own deaths in the midst of a banquet by fire and the sword and a poison commonly extracted from the yew tree."

Afterward, the Romans stationed two legions there to monitor those who remained. Archaeologists have since unearthed a well-preserved bust of Caesar Augustus in Zaragoza, a province in Tarazona, Spain.

Hispania was then divided by Caesar Augustus's general, Marcus Vipsanius Agrippa, into Lusitania, Baetica, Cantabria, and the Basque Country.

Later Roman Involvement

The Romans tended to colonize limited areas in the regions along the northern shore of Hispania after that, and there is little written history about their relations with the Basques in the Pyrenees region. Romans allowed the Basques to continue their lives as they did before, except for some limited activity on the northern coast of Hispania, which had access to the Bay of Biscay and the Celtic Sea just north of there. Most Roman interests lay in southern Hispania along the Mediterranean Sea.

Throughout ancient history, it was repeatedly said in the texts that the Basques were never entirely conquered by the Romans.

During the reign of Emperor Diocletian (284–305 CE), the Basque Country was a portion of what he called "Novempopulania," also known as "Aquitania Tertia." There was an admixture of peoples in that area, as some were of Hispanic origin, some of Basque origin, and others of French origin.

The northern areas of the Basque Country had silver mines, which were used to produce the coinage to pay the Roman troops. Archaeologists in the Basque Country have unearthed a number of these coins. They are inscribed with the word "IMON," which stood for "Barcunes," the Roman term for "Vascones." Those coins were made until 45 CE.

In 409 CE, the Vascone forces aided the Romans in fighting the Germanic barbarians— the Alans, the Suebi, and the Vandals—who had started to infiltrate the Roman Empire. In 418 CE, the Visigoths invaded. The Romans became overwhelmed by these tribes, and they drew up a treaty with the Visigoths. In exchange for driving the Alans, Suebi, and the Vandals out of Hispania, the Roman Empire awarded the Visigoths with huge segments of land in northeastern, eastern, and southeastern Hispania that they could settle.

Although there wasn't heavy colonization in the land of the Basques, there are many historic stone buildings that feature the Romanesque style of domes and gently tapered arches with hundreds of carved figures.

In 476 CE, the Western Roman Empire collapsed, and there was a scramble for the possession of the regions in the area near the Pyrenees.

Chapter 4 – Rule under Dukes, Counts, and Kings

Early Middle Age Feudal States

During the Middle Ages, the country of the Basques was generally referred to as Vasconia, after the name of its most prominent tribe. It was wedged between the Garonne River in current-day southwestern France and the Ebro River in northeastern Spain. The Ebro River runs through the Basque territory.

In 481, the Visigoths annexed some surrounding Basque areas, but they never fully conquered the entire Basque Country, which was larger back then than it is today. In 500 CE, the Visigoths controlled the tribal regions of northern Spain, southwestern Aquitaine except for the Basque Country in the northeast, and Cantabria, which was just west of there.

Evolution of the Three Duchies

The borders of today's Basque region were deeply affected by the events of the 6th century and into the Middle Ages. The borders of Francia and Hispania kept fluctuating, as Francia and the Visigoths struggled with each other.

In 507 CE, Aquitaine was still known by the Caesarian term "Gallia Aquitania." During the same year, the first king of the Franks was Clovis I. He started what was called the Merovingian dynasty. Clovis and his descendants kept dividing Gaul into smaller areas, creating instability. At that time, the Visigoths encroached at the southwestern borders of Gaul in the Basque territory.

Basque territories showing the encroachments of the Visigoths and Franks

Some smaller Gothic tribes lived in Cantabria and Vasconia. In 574 CE, King Liuvigild of the Visigoths marched against the Gothic tribes, the Cantabrians, and the Basques, invading and annexing two of the main Cantabrian towns that lay along the coast of the Bay of Biscay.

The Duchy of Cantabria

In the same year—574 CE—King Liuvigild created the Duchy of Cantabria after massacring the inhabitants. When he created Cantabria, Liuvigild absorbed some territories from the Vascones, but the Astures to the west continued to rebel. He used Cantabria as a buffer zone between the land of the Astures, which was just west of there, and the Duchy of Vasconia, which came to be called the Duchy of Gascony.

The Duchy of Gascony

In 629 CE, one of Clovis's successors, Charibert II, quelled the rebellious Basques. He had control of Aquitaine and Gascony by virtue of his marriage to Gisela, the heiress of Gascony.

Conflicts between the Visigoths, the Cantabrians, the Basques, and the Franks continued. Geographically, Gascony lay in an elbow-shaped area between modern-day France and Spain, but the borders kept shifting.

The Duchy of Aquitaine

In 602 CE, the Duchy of Aquitaine was established. In 660, Felix of Aquitaine was placed in charge of the areas within the Pyrenees, which included both the Duchy of Gascony and parts of the Duchy of Aquitaine. The Franks ruled in name only at this point, as the Duchy of Gascony was the true power in the region. Felix befriended the Basques and the Aquitanians, and he reached an agreement with them by making them *foederati*. This was an arrangement in which the overlord exchanged his protection and allegiance for military services against an enemy. At that time, the Aquitanians were permitted a degree of autonomy within Francia.

The *foederati* agreement was exercised by a later successor of Felix, Odo the Great. He became the duke of Aquitaine in 700 CE under the Frankish Merovingian dynasty. In the Battle of Toulouse in 721 CE, the Basques fended off the Saracens (Muslims) of the Umayyad dynasty, who were led by Abdul al-Rahman al-Ghafiqi. That earned Odo the epithet "the Great." Despite that title, Odo did lose possession of the historical Basque province of Sobrarbe in 724 CE. Today, that territory is part of Aragon in Spain.

When the Muslim threat accelerated, the famous Frankish leader Charles "The Hammer" Martel swung through Aquitaine, joined up with Odo the Great, and confronted the Muslims at Tours in 732 CE.

Al-Ghafiqi was killed, and his army dispersed. The Battle of Tours was a Frankish/Aquitanian victory, and it is historically significant, as it kept the Muslims out of Gaul. It is interesting to note that the Muslims underplayed the role of that victory in their histories.

However, the Western world saw it as a triumph of Christianity over Islam. In truth, it had only occurred in Francia. That arrangement continued under Odo's son and successor, Hunald I, Duke of Aquitaine.

Hunald was succeeded by his son, Waiofer (also spelled as Waiofar or Waifer), in 745. In the meantime, Charles Martel and the Frankish leaders were anxious to unite all of these duchies under a single monarchy. After the death of Charles Martel, his sons, Carloman and Pepin the Short, schemed to wrench the Duchy of Aquitaine away from Waiofer. Pepin asked Carloman to help him obtain Aquitaine. Carloman refused, so Pepin himself rallied an army to defeat Waiofer.

When Waiofer wanted to negotiate peace, Pepin ignored him, saying he had confiscated Church lands to which he had no right, and marched to Aquitaine. Waiofer then recruited some of his own French supporters, along with the Basque tribes. According to a contemporary historical source, *The Chronicle of Fredegar*, in 765 CE, Waiofer went up against Pepin "with a great army and many Vascones [Gascons] from across the Garonne, who in antiquity were called Vaceti [Basques]."

At that point, Pepin seized many of the territories of Aquitaine, devastated the vineyards, and burnt the villas he encountered. In 766 CE, Waiofer's own men deserted him. However, the unrest continued. Waiofer's family was captured and executed. Pepin suggested to Waiofer's own men that they kill him, which they did in 768 CE. Pepin also died in 768, but before doing so, he left the task of dealing with the remnants of the rebellion to his two sons, Charles I, later known as Charlemagne, and Carloman I. Although Charlemagne asked for Carloman's help, none was forthcoming, but he managed quite well without it. Charlemagne marched his army in and took over the rest of Aquitaine. The son of Waiofer, Hunald II, had taken refuge in Gascony and was under the protection of Lupus, Duke of Gascony. Charlemagne demanded that Lupus end that protection. Terrified of the mighty Charlemagne, Lupus seized Hunald II along with his wife and handed them over to Charlemagne. He then paid homage to Charlemagne.

Autonomy was important to the Aquitanians, but it was lost in 769 CE, as the province yielded to Frankish suzerainty.

Charlemagne

In late 771, Carloman I died, and the kingdom of Francia came under the sole rule of his brother, Charlemagne. Charlemagne then assigned the Duchy of Aquitaine and the Duchy of Gascony to his son, Louis. There were numerous rebellions in Gascony due in no small part to the resurrected unrest by the Basques, who resented Frank domination, and by the nearby Muslim dynasty of Banu Qasi. Their territory lay just south of Gascony in the upper Ebro River valley. The Banu Qasi was from the Muwallad dynasty, who were of mixed ancestry but had married into the Muslims or were under their influence. The Muwallads were a part of the Umayyad Emirate at Córdoba.

Pamplona was the capital city of the Duchy of Gascony, and it was inhabited by the Basques and Muslims. There was some strife there, but a moderate degree of tolerance was practiced within Pamplona between the Muslims and the Basques. That was due to the efforts of Charlemagne's predecessor, Pepin the Short. Pepin had made a pact with the Muslims to allow Christianity in Pamplona as long as the Christians paid the jizya, a special tax paid to the Emirate of Córdoba. The Emirate of Córdoba was the Muslim administration that controlled most of Spain.

Charlemagne's Disaster

In order to enforce Christianity upon these people, Charlemagne first tore down the walls of Pamplona and then nearly destroyed the city. Both Christian and Muslim Basques were outraged and planned revenge. Religion wasn't an issue for the Basques; however, the occupation of their territory was.

In an effort to expand his Frankish empire into Muslim Spain, Charlemagne attacked Zuberoa in 778 CE. Zuberoa is the historical Basque province of Soule. It was (and is) a Basque province. The Muslims had the Basques, who had been forcefully converted to Christianity, as their allies. Charlemagne met up with the Basques at the treacherous Roncevaux Pass. This was a narrow mountain path with an elevation of 3,500 feet. The Basques, who were veteran mountain fighters, separated the rearguard of the Frankish forces along with their supplies. According to the *Annales regni Francorum* (the *Royal Frankish Annals*), "The Franks were superior to the Vascones [Basques] both in armament and in courage, but the roughness of the terrain and the difference in the style of combat made them [the Franks] generally weaker."

The rearguard that had been left behind earlier in the battle were slaughtered "to the last man," at least according to later medieval historians. Charlemagne's well-known fighter, Roland, also died during this military disaster. This great battle was memorialized in the poem *The Song of Roland*. It laments France's loss, spoken as if through the mouth of Roland: "O land of France, O blissful pleasant land, today laid desolate by such cruel waste! Brave French, I see you die on my account, and I unable to protect your lives." Scholars believe it was written by the French-Norman poet Turold between 1040 and 1115.

An anonymous Basque poet wrote of the same battle from the Basque point of view: "What were they in our hills, these Northern men? Why come they here to our quiet land? God made the hills intending for none should pass...Streams of red blood! Quivers among the mangled flesh! Oh! What a sea of blood! What shattered bones!" And he later added the verse that identified the battle with Roland at Roncevaux Pass: "Fly, Charlemagne, red cloak and raven plumes! Lies thy stout nephew, Roland, stark in death; for him his brilliant courage naught avails." This poem was found in the year 1794 in a convent in Fuentarrabía (often known as Hondarribia in English) in the Basque Country.

Charlemagne endured a huge setback at his defeat at Roncevaux Pass, as he had intended to proceed unimpaired through the rest of Hispania, which was mostly controlled by the Muslim Emirate of Córdoba.

In the 8th century, the Franks struggled against the Muslim invaders, who were intent upon conquering all of current-day Spain. The relationship between the Basques and the Muslims was a rocky one, and the two parties vacillated between peace and war. During that time, a segment of the Basque population, especially those who lived in the Ebro River Valley, adopted a form of Islam. The Basques who lived in the northern area of the Ebro Valley, however, were not converted, and they continued to practice Christianity or their ancient pagan religion. Although the Franks had control, their efforts were short-lived. In 812, the Franks under Louis the Pious once again fought against the Emirate of Córdoba.

In 816 CE, at the Battle of Pancorbo, the Basque king, Velasco the Basque, had the support of the Franks and also received aid from the Kingdom of Asturias, which was founded by the Visigoths in 718. All of them went up against Abd al-Karim ibn Abd al-Wahid at Pancorbo, an area full of fords, rivers, ravines, and mountain passes through the Pyrenees. The battle raged for thirteen days. The rivers were loaded up with logs, making them impossible to navigate. When the Christian Basque troops tried to cross the river, they were massacred by the Muslims. Many others died falling off the steep cliffs. The Muslims won, but the Basques staged more revolts, which were mostly directed against their Frankish overlords.

After this fateful battle, the Basque leader, Íñigo Arista, fostered the rebuilding of the city and the fortifications at Pamplona, starting in 790 CE.

Chapter 5 – The Middle Ages

Navarre

In 824 CE, Íñigo Arista was elected as the king of Pamplona, partially due to his deeds in the Battle of Pancorbo. He was Christian, but his half-brother, Musa ibn Musa of the Banu Qasi, was Muslim and permitted Arista to control the city of Pamplona as long as they paid the jizya, the taxes charged to non-Muslims. There were occasional rebellions there between Christian and Muslim forces, but Íñigo's objective was to establish a Basque state that wouldn't be subservient to the domination of the Emirate of Córdoba or the Franks. That state would be the Kingdom of Navarre.

After Íñigo died in 851, his remains were buried in the Romanesque-style monastery of Leyre in what is now San Salvador, Navarre.

His half-brother, Musa ibn Musa, took over Navarre, and Arista's son, García Íñiguez I, was made the king of Pamplona. In Navarre, many of the nobles defected to the Emirate of Córdoba. Absent of a popular power base, Musa also defected as well. During 851, Musa had to deal with an insurrection by the Basques. The Basques allied themselves with the Kingdom of Asturias but were defeated at the

Battle of Albelda. Musa then threw the Basque and Asturian leaders into a dungeon.

By 854 CE, Musa took control of the provinces of Zaragoza, Huesca, Tudela, and Toledo. He was then referred to as the "Third King of Hispania."

Later, possibly in 860, another battle was waged against the Muslims by the Basque king of Pamplona, García Íñiguez, and King Ordoño I of Asturias. It was said the Muslims were defeated at the Battle of Monte Laturce and forced to flee. Over time, facts surrounding that battle were adapted as a backdrop for the legendary battle called the Battle of Clavijo. It is steeped in an old Christian legend and states that James, Jesus Christ's apostle, appeared at Clavijo and led the Christians to victory.

After García passed away, the area was restive, as his eldest son and successor, Fortún Garcés, was weak. Before the end of Fortún's reign, Sancho Garcés received the aid of Alfonso III of the Asturians and assumed control in 905 CE, ending the Íñiguez dynasty.

Sancho was strictly anti-Muslim and worked to expel the Emirate of Córdoba from the Kingdom of Navarre. In 911 CE, a former ally of his, Galindo Aznárez II, allied himself with two Muslim lords, Abd Allah ibn Lubb and Muhammad al-Tawil. They attacked Sancho but were defeated. Muhammad fled, and it is assumed that ibn Lubb fled with him. Galindo was forced to become a vassal. Little by little, the Muslim territories in that area were shrinking.

In 918, Sancho allied with Ordoño II of León to flush out the Muslims from the Upper March, which lay in the Ebro Valley. They conquered the towns of Calahorra, Arnedo, and Viguera from the Banu Quasi. Though they failed to capture the municipality of Valtierra, they did burn down the mosque there. The son of Muhammad al-Tawil, Amrus ibn Muhammad, wanted to set up his own private kingdom, so Sancho and his allies joined together to oust the Banu Qasi-held territory of Monzón. This allowed Sancho to expand his dominion into Lower Navarre.

The Battle of Calatañazor

In 1002, more Muslims entered Hispania. They were called the "Saracens" by medieval historians, as they lacked detailed information about the various caliphates in the Arab world. The Christian forces fought under Alfonso V of León, a Spanish province; Sancho III of Navarre; and Count Sancho García of Castile. The Muslims were led by Almanzor. He may not have held the title of a ruler, but he was definitely the one with the power in the Umayyad Caliphate of Córdoba, the ruling body that had replaced the former Emirate of Córdoba.

The Battle of Calatañazor was a major battle in the campaign by the Christians to expel the Muslims out of the province of Castile in Spain. This day-long battle occurred in the province of Calatañazor, which straddled both Castile and León. In preparation for this battle, Almanzor recruited troops from North Africa. There were thousands of troops who participated. In the end, Almanzor and his forces were defeated. Almanzor was wounded, but history indicates that he continued to wage war against the Christians in Spain. Eventually, he came upon a castle fortress manned by Christian warriors. There, he was defeated. Almanzor's health declined due to the wounds he incurred at Calatañazor, and he became more debilitated. As he lay dying, he said to his son, "This appears to me the first sign of the decadence that awaits the empire." According to a local legend, a mysterious fisherman appeared in another town and said, "In Calatañazor, Almanzor lost the drum." This was believed to be the lament of the devil when his demons failed to prevail over the forces of good.

Sancho Garcés III: Sancho the Great

During the 9ᵗʰ century, the Kingdom of Navarre grew in prestige and importance. In Basque history, Sancho Garcés III is featured as one of the country's greatest unifiers and one of its most important kings, which is why he inherited his nickname "the Great." In 1004, he was the king of Pamplona. Through marriage, he came to rule the County of Castile, along with the feudal states of Álava and Monzón.

Under Sancho's successors, the Kingdom of Navarre was divided into Castile, Pamplona, and the Basque provinces of Ribagorza, Sobrarbe, and the new province of Aragon. These areas had expanded under Sancho Garcés to include not only the lowlands but also the urban centers. Because of that, the Basques intermingled with the French, causing a predominance of French- and Spanish-speaking people. Due to this, the Basque language became the language of the minority. This is why some of the regions of the Basque Country today speak only *Euskara*, while other regions speak a mixture of Basque, Spanish, and French.

García Sánchez III

Sancho III made arrangements with his sons before his death in terms of their inheritances. García III was the eldest son of Sancho III, and as such, he was to inherit the kingship of Navarre (Pamplona) and would have control of Álava and Gipuzkoa. His brother, Ferdinand I, was to have control over part of the County of Castile, while García III would oversee the other, larger portion of Castile. Ramiro I received the County of Aragon, and Gonzalo was given the rulership over the Basque territories of Sobrarbe and Ribagorza.

After Gonzalo died unexpectedly in 1043, Ramiro was awarded Aragon, Sobrarbe, and Ribagorza. At that time, Ribagorza and Sobrarbe were assimilated into the Spanish province of Aragon. Upon Ramiro's death, his son, Sancho Ramírez, had control of Navarre (Pamplona) and Aragon. Sancho Ramírez then called himself "King of the Aragonese and Pamplonese." He was the first to proclaim himself King of Aragon.

"Emperor" Ferdinand

In 1037, García Sánchez III and Ferdinand I went to war with the Kingdom of León, a Spanish territory just west of Pamplona. By that time, it included much of the territory once belonging to the Kingdom of Asturias. García and Ferdinand defeated King Bermudo III of León, who was killed in the battle. Ferdinand then became the king of León, as well as the count of Castile. However, in time, the brothers argued about the distribution of the lands of León, Castile, and Pamplona. In 1054, Ferdinand battled his brother at the ancient mountains near Atapuerca, and García was killed.

García Sánchez's son, Sancho, was the legitimate heir of the estate, as inheritances were passed along to the direct descendants. Sancho was only fourteen in 1054, so his mother, Stephanie, was the regent. Sancho was crowned king of Pamplona and became Sancho Garcés IV immediately after his father's death.

Ferdinand was said to have called himself "emperor," basing that on the charters of Aragon drawn up in 1056, which says Ferdinand was the "emperor in León and in Castile." Ferdinand's consort was Queen Sancha, the sister of deceased King Bermudo III of León, which may have been interpreted as strengthening Ferdinand's claim.

Ferdinand took advantage of Sancho and reduced Navarre (Pamplona) to the status of a vassal state. Ferdinand was ambitious. He captured Zaragoza in 1060 CE, which, at that time, was under Muslim control. The emir was then made to pay tribute to Ferdinand.

Ferdinand craved the territory of Toledo, so he attacked its two neighboring cities, Talamanca and Alcalá de Henares, and conquered them. The emir of Toledo, Yahya ibn Ismail al-Mamun, wanted to avoid the destruction of Toledo, so he submitted himself to Ferdinand.

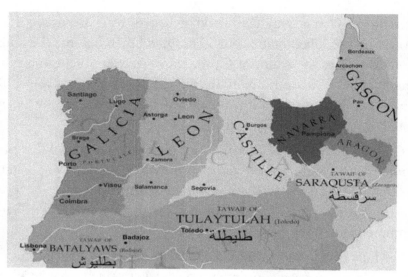

*The Iberian Peninsula with its 11ᵗʰ-century Provinces
and those of Francia*

In 1063, Ferdinand continued to expand his territories in Spain and raided the Muslim states of Badajoz and Seville. He raided them as a scare tactic, and the Muslim rulers agreed to pay tribute to him to avoid future raids. Although it was a form of extortion, this was a common practice in those days.

In 1065, Ferdinand invaded Valencia. Before Ferdinand could reach the heart of the territory, Emir Abd al-Malik al-Muzaffar submitted to him, agreeing to pay tribute.

The Death of Ferdinand

Like his father, Ferdinand decided to make arrangements for the inheritances of his children before he died.

Even though Alfonso VI wasn't his eldest son, Ferdinand chose to bequeath the Kingdom of León to him. Sancho II, also known as Sancho "the Strong," who was the eldest, received Pamplona and the Kingdom of Castile, along with the rights to the tributes given by the Muslim ruler of Zaragoza. Ferdinand's youngest male heir, García II, was originally supposed to receive the Kingdom of Galicia, and he also obtained the lands that lay on the northwestern coast of Spain and Navarre. The territory of Galicia was unstable until Ferdinand's younger daughter, Elvira, was given the city of Toro and half of the income of the monasteries within Ferdinand's lands. His other daughter, Urraca, was to receive the monastic income and the city of Zamora. Arrangements for the income from the monastic lands was only valid as long as the women were unmarried.

Ferdinand became deathly ill during his siege of Valencia and decided to return home to León, which he had confiscated earlier. He died there in 1065.

El Cid and Sancho II

Sancho II decided to recruit Rodrigo Díaz de Vivar, an accomplished knight, to help him challenge Alfonso for possession of León. Rodrigo was also called El Cid by the Muslim Moors, whom he had dealings with as part of his service to the kings and nobles in Spain.

El Cid helped Sancho II defeat Alfonso at the Battle of Golpejera in 1072. After that, Alfonso was arrested. For some reason, Sancho II decided to spare his brother. Alfonso was exiled to the city of Toledo, which was in the hands of a Muslim king. Sancho II then became the king of León and Castile.

El Cid also helped Sancho lay siege to the city of Zamora, which was held by his sister Urraca. In a strange twist of fate, a nobleman by the name of Vellido Adolfo was hired to assassinate Sancho II. He lured Sancho into meeting with him privately, saying that he knew of a weakness in the Castle of Zamora. When Sancho rounded the corner of the castle, Vellido stabbed him. El Cid gave chase, but Vellido slipped out of the city through a gateway and vanished. Today, that gateway is called *Portillo del Traidor* or, in English, "Gateway of the Traitor."

After his father's murder, Sancho IV inherited the rights to Pamplona. Sancho was also crowned as the king of Pamplona (Navarre). Likewise, he was the count of Álava, Bureba, Gipuzkoa,

Biscay, and Alta Rioja. However, in 1076, he was assassinated by his jealous siblings at a promontory in Navarre.

With the death of Sancho IV, Alfonso VI became the king of León and Castile, and he also gained Sancho IV's territories of Navarre, Álava, Bureba, Gipuzkoa, Biscay, and Alta Rioja. An issue arose regarding the kingship of Navarre. To resolve the crisis, it was decided that Navarre would be divided between Alfonso VI and Sancho V Ramírez. In the end, part of Navarre was in Castile, and the other portion was in Aragon.

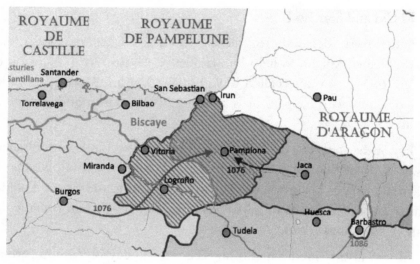

Basque territories under assault

Civil War

Alfonso VI had no male heirs, so he tried to arrange for a successor. He legitimatized his mistress, Zaida, in order to have a male heir. She was a Muslim princess, and they had a son together. Zaida converted to Catholicism and was renamed "Isabel." In 1103, Alfonso met with his councilors and named his only son, Sancho Alfónsez, as his heir presumptive. Alfonso's carefully laid succession plan went awry when Sancho went to war against the Muslim Almoravids of Toledo, for he lost the Battle of Uclés in 1107. After the battle, Sancho was on the run. He was killed by villagers in 1108.

Alfonso VI was desperate. Not wanting his lands to fall into the hands of his rivals, Alfonso made his widowed daughter, Urraca, the heir presumptive. To seal her right to the throne, the Leonese and Castilian nobles insisted she marry. Alfonso objected to the suitors they presented, as they could become fierce rivals. He selected King Alfonso I of Aragon around 1109. Alfonso I was the son of Sancho V Ramírez, making Urraca and Alfonso second cousins. That way, everything stayed "within the family," so to speak. However, that became a problem later on.

Alfonso the "Battler" and a Woman's Wiles

Alfonso was noted for his military prowess, and he was said to have won "twenty-nine" battles. He also fought alongside El Cid in Valencia. For his efforts, his father, Sancho V Ramírez, awarded him with the rulership of Ardennes, Luna, Bailo, and Biel.

Alfonso's marriage was performed for political reasons. Urraca's father, Alfonso VI, had caveats attached to their marriage contract. First of all, the contract indicated that if either party left the other without a mutual agreement, he or she would forfeit the support of their followers. Neither of them could leave the other because of their familiar relationship to each other or for fear of excommunication by the pope.

Furthermore, if Urraca gave birth to a male, that child would inherit both Alfonso's and Urraca's properties. In the case that Urraca had no male child, her properties would be bequeathed to her successors, not his. If Urraca died first, her properties would be awarded to her son by her prior marriage, Alfonso Raimúndez.

In 1110, Alfonso and Urraca separated. Alfonso had been a bachelor for many years, and it was said he preferred the company of men to women, though there's no indication this was true. It would seem, though, that he had difficulty relating to women, especially his ambitious wife.

Alfonso claimed total control of Castile, León, Toledo, and Aragon. In 1114, their marriage was annulled for reasons of consanguinity. Of course, that meant their marriage contract was null and void, but Alfonso still held on to his lands. Urraca was nearly as militaristic as her husband. She raised her own troops and marched against Alfonso. Her forces attacked Castile, but Alfonso, who was anxious to return to his conquests of the Muslim lands in Spain, made a truce with Urraca.

Alfonso the "Battler"

Urraca later became involved in a conflict with Bishop Diego Gelmírez of Galicia. The bishop had appointed a guardian, Pedro Fróilaz de Traba, for Urraca's underage son, Alfonso Raimúndez. De Trada was a highly politicized figure in Galicia and detested Urraca and her high-handed ways. In 1121, Urraca made the colossal error of arresting the bishop in retaliation for the selection of de Traba. When threatened with excommunication by Pope Callixtus II, Urraca immediately made amends. Otherwise, she would have lost control of all her holdings.

Urraca died in 1126, and her son and heir, Alfonso VII (Alfonso Raimúndez), started a campaign to regain all of the territories that had been lost to Alfonso the Battler.

Peace of Támara

In 1127, Alfonso I the Battler made an agreement with the younger Alfonso to determine the possessions within Castile and Aragon. They agreed Alfonso I would be the ruler of Biscay, Gipuzkoa, Belorado, Soria, Buerba, San Esteban de Gormaz, and Alta Rioja.

By doing this, they reverted the border of Castile to its original borders of 1054. In return, Alfonso I recognized Alfonso VII as the king of Castile.

Battle of Fraga

In 1134, Alfonso I the Battler sent his forces from Aragon and the neighboring city of Barcelona to conquer the Muslim-held areas in the lowlands leading to the Ebro River Valley. The Muslim forces, which numbered 2,700 knights, besieged the town of Fraga in Aragon. Alfonso clashed with the cavalry sent by the emir of Murcia when they arrived on the scene. The battle dragged on. When the emir of Córdoba sent in more forces, they decimated Alfonso's troops. The beaten Alfonso then gathered up the survivors and fled to a district of Zaragoza. Alfonso I died of his wounds several days later.

The Crisis over Navarre and Castile

After the deaths of Alfonso I and Urraca, there was a succession crisis. For about half a century, Navarre had been divided between Castile and Aragon. After Alfonso I died, he left his properties to the Knights Templar, the Hospitallers, and the Knights of the Holy Sepulchre. All three of these were semi-religious orders. The nobility of Aragon objected to this, though. In order to resolve the issue, they looked back at the line of succession. A convocation of nobles decided that Ramiro II, Alfonso I's brother The Navarrese nobles sought out García Ramírez, who was the great-grandson of Sancho III. García Ramírez was also known as García the Restorer because he restored independence to Navarre, which had been joined to Aragon for decades.

The issue of the other Basque districts that had been seized by Alfonso I the Battler, and subsequently by his son, Alfonso VII, wasn't yet resolved. García Ramírez fought with Castile over its western lands. Alfonso VII and García made a pact in which the historic Basque districts of Álava, Biscay, Gipuzkoa, and Alta Rioja would be returned. However, Alfonso never kept the agreement. Regardless, Alfonso continued to let Navarre retain much of its self-government. He did that in order to obtain their favor. The viceroys of the towns swore to uphold their traditional charters, and in exchange, Navarre agreed to cede La Rioja to Castile.

However, the successive kings of Castile worked on granting the people in those territories, including Navarre, a high level of self-government. In fact, other towns and districts in Castile gained a limited state of autonomy under charters later called *fueros*. When trade routes were more firmly established, towns were able to secure charters by which they could operate as semi-independent provinces. Castile permitted those provinces to pass their own laws and keep their own customs.

"Tall" Sancho

The son of Sancho VI (the son and successor of García Ramírez) and Sancha (the daughter of Alfonso VII of León and Castile) was Sancho VII. He became the king of Navarre in 1194. A forensic anthropologist recently discovered that Sancho VII was over seven feet tall, which must have made an impression on the people around him. In 1212, he joined forces with the neighboring Christian provinces to expel the Muslims. It was said that Sancho's Basque soldiers carried shields emblazoned with a star symbol, which represented the Sun of Death or possibly the Christian symbol of life and death.

Sancho's sisters were Berengaria and Blanche. Berengaria was married to Richard the Lionheart of England, and it was said that Sancho and the English king were fairly close. Blanche died in 1229, and Berengaria passed in 1230. When Sancho died in 1234, he had no heirs. Since he had no siblings left to give the throne to, Navarre went to Blanche's son, Theobald IV, Count of Champagne. This transfer was supported by the Navarrese nobility.

King Theobald I of Navarre

In 1234, Count Theobald IV of Champagne became Theobald I, King of Navarre. Since he hailed from a foreign territory, he knew nothing about the Basques.

King Theobald came to understand that the Basques were unique and different from their Indo-European neighbors, and he developed the first written charters, or *fueros*, to promote smooth relations with the monarchy of Navarre and the Basque people. In 1238, he drew up the first *Fuero General de Navarra* ("General Charter of Navarre"). This charter defined the distribution of powers among the king, the courts, and the parliament (called the *Cortes*), which represented the people. The Basques maintained their customs and had a set of laws for themselves, but those laws were really common laws delivered orally throughout the ages. Theobald's direct successor, Theobald II, upheld the policies of his father. His son, Henry I, also confirmed the *fueros* of Navarre.

While there was a mix of languages spoken over the years in the Basque Country, *Euskara*, the traditional Basque language, was mainly spoken. In some of the areas, Spanish and French were also used. The Basques often called the non-Basque speaking population "Gascons," after the historical term "Vascones."

Chapter 6 – The Late Middle Ages

Autonomy/Home Rule in the French Basque Country

The representative assemblies, called the Juntas Generales, represented the Basque population in France, with its provinces of Labourd, Soule, and Lower Navarre. (Upper Navarre is located in Spain.)

Hostilities Build

In 1285, King Theobald's granddaughter, Joan I, became the queen of Navarre. She never visited Navarre and instead put it in the hands of French governors, who were very unpopular. Philip IV of France, Joan's wife, retained the kingdom of Navarre for France.

The throne of France and Navarre eventually fell into the hands of Philip V (in Navarre, he was known as Philip II). Some of the English holdings in France had been transferred to the royalty in England by virtue of marriage, which only helped to contribute to the friction between England and France. Philip V ruled Navarre from 1316 to 1322. He saw to it that women could not succeed to the throne, and he was succeeded by Charles IV, his brother (known as Charles I in Navarre).

Edward II, the king of England, was also the duke of Aquitaine and had territories in Gascony. He was expected to pay homage to King Charles IV. However, he delayed because of some conspiracies at home. In retribution, Charles IV confiscated some of Edward's lands. In order to resolve the situation, Edward appealed to Pope John XXII. The pope contacted Charles, who agreed to return some of the lands if Edward paid homage. Aware of the difficulties Edward had in England, the pope made arrangements for Edward's wife, Isabella, to serve as an ambassador. To maintain control, royal families frequently intermarried. As it so happened, Isabella was also Charles IV's sister.

Upon her arrival, Isabella and Charles made a truce. The truce specified that the French lands would be returned with the exception of a small portion of land called Agenais if Isabella's son, Prince Edward, would pay him homage on behalf of his father. After Prince Edward arrived, he paid homage, but Charles didn't return the Aquitaine properties. However, France could resume control of its other lands there.

That wasn't satisfactory. Isabella was a schemer who almost always got what she wanted. She was dubbed as the "She-Wolf" of France because of that. This time, she wanted the reacquisition of Aquitaine. Besides, she wanted to stay in France so she could pursue a relationship with Roger Mortimer, an exiled Englishman. Her son, Edward, was with her, so she decided to betroth him to Philippa, the daughter of a local count. Marriage with royals of another territory would come in handy for her scheme.

She then decided to invade England with a mercenary army. She had the powerful duke of Lancaster, with an entourage of bishops, present her husband, Edward II, with two options: 1) abdicate the throne in favor of his son, or 2) have his son disinherited (in which case the throne would go to an alternate candidate). Faced with that choice, Edward reluctantly abdicated.

When some of the notables in the kingdom saw these machinations, they tried to go to his rescue. Rapidly, Mortimer sequestered the miserable Edward II in Berkeley Castle. In 1327, he died. The timing seemed rather convenient, but no one could prove that any foul play was involved.

Charles IV died in 1328, but he had no male heirs. He was succeeded by his niece, Joan II of Navarre, and his cousin, Philip VI of Valois. Edward III of England was expected to return and pay homage to Philip. He did so, but he offended the French by failing to remove his crown at the ceremony.

Further friction occurred when France supported the Kingdom of Scotland in their resistance to England. For years, the English monarchs wanted to conquer Scotland. Once France gave its allegiance to Scotland, King Edward III knew he couldn't succeed in gaining control over the Scots.

Tensions grew between England and France. England had given refuge to Robert III of Artois, a devious English nobleman who fled France when charged with forgery. In 1336, France demanded his extradition, but England refused. Tensions between both countries were at a fever pitch.

Artois used this animosity to his own advantage. He grabbed the ear of young Edward III and reminded him that he had the right to claim the throne of France through his marriage to Philippa of Hainault. She was descended from Charles of Valois, the father of King Philip VI of France.

The Hundred Years' War

Because of his familial connections to the royalty of France, Edward III of England formally declared himself "King of France and the French royal arms" in 1340. In 1346, the English army under Edward III landed in Normandy, and it plowed a path of destruction across northern France. In August of 1346, the two armies met at Crécy. They moved southward and reached the River Seine. The English longbowmen were Edward's most effective division. They wiped out the French forces they encountered and moved up toward Calais, along the northern coast of France.

Philip VI died in 1350, which was around the same time the Black Plague hit France and England. Troops, especially those of France, were decimated by the disease. Philip's successor, John II, continued the struggle.

In Poitiers, Edward III's son, Edward, better known as Edward the Black Prince of Wales, led his army from Gascony and continued plundering. With the aid of a Gascon noble, Jean III de Grailly, Prince Edward met up with King John II's army in 1356. John II was actually captured and taken prisoner, making France kingless. The French Dauphin, who was the heir presumptive, and England tried to negotiate a settlement. After several years, the Treaty of Brétigny was signed. A huge ransom was to be paid for the release of King John II, and Edward III renounced his claim on the French throne. Furthermore, John was required to send his younger son, Louis, Duke of Anjou, as a hostage. In exchange, France would cede Aquitaine to England. Louis of Anjou later escaped, and John II returned to England as a hostage. He felt dishonored by the actions of his son and wanted to keep to the terms that had been agreed upon. He died in prison (although it should be noted he lived fairly nicely for a prisoner and was treated with great respect) and was succeeded by Charles V.

In Spain, there was a dispute over the provinces of Castile and Aragon. That became an issue, as Charles V recruited allies from Castile. Thus, both England and France became embroiled in the Castilian Civil War.

The Castilian Civil War

In Spain, King Peter was the ruler of Castile and León. However, his half-brother, Henry of Trastámara, who lived in France at the time, laid claim to the throne. With the support of Charles V of France, Henry gathered an army of French soldiers. He also had help from the Black Prince of England and a soldier of fortune named

Bertrand du Guesclin. In exchange for the Black Prince's aid, Henry of Trastámara agreed to help defray the costs of the battle. With their massive army, they attacked Peter. He was deposed and was forced to flee.

Henry of Trastámara then returned to Castile in 1368 to a rousing welcome. He was supported as the king of Castile by the local nobles.

However, Peter had not given up. In 1369, Peter of Castile again confronted Henry at the fortress of Montiel. Henry besieged the fort and prevailed. Henry's envoy, Bertrand du Guesclin, met Peter to discuss terms. Peter promised to pay Bertrand 200,000 gold coins and the towns of Soria, Atienza, and Almazan if he betrayed Henry of Trastámara. When Bertrand returned, he told Henry of the offer, using it to his advantage to get paid more by Henry, who, of course, wanted Peter gone. Bertrand then returned to Peter and led him to his tent, in which Henry was hiding. Henry didn't immediately recognize Peter, as they had not seen each other in a long time. When Peter identified himself, Henry attacked him with a knife, and Peter fell to the ground. Then Henry stabbed him numerous times and left him unburied for three days. Thus, Henry (now Henry II) became the king of Castile and León.

After the death of Charles V of France in 1380, Charles VI ascended to the throne. However, Charles was mentally ill, and the duke of Orléans and the duke of Burgundy descended into their own civil war. Duke John of Burgundy was killed in 1419.

England took advantage of the internal conflicts in France by stepping up their attacks under Henry V. In 1415, Henry crossed into Normandy. The French forces pursued him, but Henry defeated them at the Battle of Agincourt. The French were unprepared to go up against Henry's much larger force, and about 6,000 French soldiers were killed.

Philip, who became Duke of Burgundy after his father's death, wanted to put an end to the constant hostilities. He proposed that Henry V of England marry Charles VI's daughter, Catherine. That way, Catherine would be an heir to the French throne, and Henry could act as her regent. Upon the death of King Charles VI, the French crown would go to Henry's heirs. That would yield a dual monarchy—that of England and France. In 1420, this was agreed to in what is known as the Treaty of Troyes.

Catherine and Henry V gave birth to Henry VI in 1421. When both Charles VI and Henry V died in 1422, the treaty was essentially tossed out the window. Although the throne should have gone to Henry VI, Dauphin Charles of France claimed it as his own. He ran into many difficulties and soon found himself on the losing side of the war.

The famous Joan of Arc inspired the Dauphin not to give up hope. She herself led the French forces in the Battle of Orléans, which was a rousing success. After that, the Dauphin marched to Rheims, where he was crowned King Charles VII of France.

As one might expect, England didn't recognize this claim. In Compiégne, Joan was captured and sent to England for trial. She was convicted of heresy and was burned at the stake in 1431.

Joan of Arc's execution

Despite this setback, France went on to win the war in 1453. Not much changed for the Basques, although if the English had won, things most certainly would have.

Spanish Conquest of Navarre

Two noble families, the Beaumonts and the Agramonts, fought over control of Navarre and created problems in the Basque Country. In 1484, the control of Navarre was hotly contested, as the French portion of it lay on the northern section of the Pyrenees, where the Beaumonts were established, and the southern portion lay on the southern section, which was in Spain, where the Agramonts lived. Disagreements between the Spanish and French nobles ensued over control of Navarre. King Ferdinand II, who controlled Aragon and Castile through his marriage to Queen Isabella I, wanted to claim all of Navarre as a Spanish territory.

In 1504, Queen Isabella died. Her successor was her daughter, Joanna. Joanna was often called Joanna the Mad because of her severe mental instability. Although she was the ruling monarch of Castile, she was placed in a royal convent at Tordesillas by her father, Ferdinand II of Aragon. Joanna had a son named Charles, but he wasn't of age, so Ferdinand was his regent.

In 1512, Ferdinand joined the "Holy League," which was formed by Pope Julius II, who named France as an enemy to the interests of the papacy. For Ferdinand, this was merely a way to justify attacking northern Navarre. In 1512, Ferdinand organized a Spanish military force in the Basque province of Gipuzkoa and attacked Navarre, conquering the fortifications there. Ferdinand's force was huge, and the Beaumonts had to retreat.

The Castilian troops, manned mostly by soldiers from Gipuzkoa, crossed the Pyrenees via its passes. Once they arrived, they confiscated or destroyed the buildings belonging to the Beaumont faction. Ferdinand and his forces marched to the walls of the capital city of Pamplona, where he insisted the inhabitants swear allegiance to him. Pamplona capitulated, and Ferdinand then stationed his troops throughout the area. Ferdinand further demanded that John III of Navarre swear allegiance to him and send his young heir apparent, Henry, to the Castilian court to be raised there. John III and his wife, Catherine, refused. Instead, they fled and sought refuge in the neighboring province of Béarn.

Ferdinand made many efforts to justify his right to assume control of Navarre by obtaining papal support. Ferdinand offered concessions and agreed to respect Navarrese laws. The status of Navarre shifted in 1512 when Ferdinand was appointed king of Navarre.

Two Navarrese Counterattacks

John III, the former king of Navarre, saw his chance to retake Navarre after the death of Ferdinand in January 1516. So, John organized a military force of mostly Vascone soldiers. They took a number of prisoners, including some members of the Agramont family. However, John III's military failed to gain total control of the French area of Navarre.

Spain was in an economic downturn at that time, and Francis I of France jumped at the opportunity to gain control of Navarre. However, he was not the only one. Henry II, the son of John III and Catherine, was living in exile in Béarn. He was the rightful heir to the Kingdom of Navarre, and he gathered an army of 12,000 Vascones and displaced Navarrese to fight for his rightful throne.

Ignatius Loyola and the Battle of Pamplona

Ignatius Loyola, the future founder of the Jesuits, was initially a military man. Ignatius, or Íñigo in the Basque language, was born in the Basque province of Gipuzkoa. He was an expert swordsman and somewhat violent in his youth. He even had duels with other men, sometimes over issues related to his Catholic beliefs.

In 1521, Ignatius served as the Castilian military governor of Pamplona, the capital of Navarre. His commander, Antonio Manrique de Lara, 2nd Duke of Nájera, and his forces were away from Pamplona, fighting a local rebellion, when the French invaded. Ignatius and his soldiers were left to defend the castle at Pamplona without any support.

Many Navarrese citizens backed the French and attacked Ignatius and his men at the castle. Ignatius and his soldiers fought bravely but were eventually defeated. During the attack, Ignatius was severely injured. His leg was shattered when it was hit with a cannonball. Even though he was on the side of Spain, the Franco-Navarrese soldiers admired Ignatius for his courage and brought him back to his home in Loyola.

Since he could no longer fight, Ignatius went on to found the Society of Jesus, whose followers are known as Jesuits, and later was made a Catholic saint. Francis Xavier was also beatified for his efforts in founding the Jesuits. He was also a Basque who hailed from Navarre.

Battle of Esquíroz (Noáin)

In June 1521, French General André de Foix saw an opportunity to seize control of Navarre because Castile was involved in an uprising by the citizens. John III's son, Henry II, then called upon the French and Navarre to take on the Spanish forces. He mustered a force of about 10,000 men. The Spanish called for volunteers, and their newly formed troops numbered 30,000! At Esquíroz, which is near Pamplona, the French forces were defeated, and General André de Foix was captured.

Fall of Amaiur

After having an insufficient number of forces in the Battle of Esquíroz, the Franco-Navarrese mustered as many as 27,000 soldiers in their expedition to regain control of Navarre and the Basque areas. Many were French forces, and the others were Gascons (Basques). They marched toward the Bidasoa River in northern Navarre and then on to Baztan, where they placed a Castilian stronghold under siege. The Castilians then surrendered in exchange for unobstructed passage back to Castile.

Under the command of Guillaume Gouffier, the combined Franco-Navarrese troops captured the fortress of Urantzu and then moved upon Hondarribia in Gipuzkoa, a Basque province along the Bidasoa River. They captured the coastal fortification there.

In 1522, Holy Roman Emperor Charles V and his Castilian-Aragon forces left Pamplona with 7,000 men and marched to the fortress of Amaiur. The Navarrese forces consisted of only 200 knights, as they were awaiting reinforcements. The relief forces never arrived, and the fort fell rapidly. The Navarrese commanders were imprisoned in Pamplona, and two were deliberately poisoned.

In 1524, the Franco-Navarrese forces were promised restitution of their properties if they vowed allegiance to Emperor Charles V, which they did. Their properties, however, weren't fully restored, which led to sporadic clashes, mostly in Lower Navarre.

Fear of Witches

The Catholic Church and the Roman papacy had a great deal of political power in Europe. Charles V, the Holy Roman Emperor, spent many years dealing with the Muslims in the Ottoman Empire and with political alliances made between the Muslims and even the Christian kings, like Francis I of France. Charles V defended the Catholic Church from the pressures of Islam and the Protestant religions during his reign. Deviations from the teachings of the Bible, as interpreted by ordained priests, were viewed as contaminations of sacred scripture, and these people were often found guilty of heresy.

King Charlemagne (r. 800–814), who had imposed Catholicism upon France, stated, "If anyone, deceived by the devil, shall believe as is customary among pagans, that any man or woman is a night-witch, and eats men, and on that account burn that person to death and he shall be executed."

In Spain, Muslims controlled many territories. In the 16th century, Spain ordered all Muslims to convert to Catholicism, although they didn't do so until a century later. Also, during the 16th century, the Protestant Reformation started in Germany, where it soon spread throughout Europe. Heresy and witchcraft were often packaged together, and people sometimes believed that Protestants believed in supernatural beings. The rationale for connecting Protestantism with witchcraft was flawed.

The Ecclesiastical Inquisition

An inquisition was a tribunal established by the papacy to prevent misguided teachings and practices from infiltrating the population. That sometimes occurred when people had converted from another religious belief to Catholicism. Such tribunals were established in the 13th century and were reaffirmed in later centuries. Initially, the Dominican order was assigned the task of holding these ecclesiastical trials, but that was later transferred to the Jesuits.

The Basque Witch Trials

In 1525, in Navarre, a special commission was established to explore the mountainous regions of Navarre where the Basques lived. They had heard rumors that people had seen the "devil's mark" on women. The devil's mark was the appearance of a red or blue mark on the body made from the claw of a demon. Investigators were dispatched and returned with about thirty individuals.

Judge Pedro de Balanza, a royal magistrate, was sent out to "inquire, learn, correct, punish, and sentence the diabolical sect and the crimes committed by these witches who are said to be in this Kingdom of Navarra." Two girls, aged nine and eleven, came forward claiming to be "witch-finders." The number of people convicted is unknown, but judgment was said to have been swift, resulting in executions. Modern estimates believe about fifty were executed.

In 1534, an odd woman by the name of Maria Sagardoy was accused on the basis that she kept a dead toad on her porch. Her story was embroidered to the point that it was reported that she made concoctions and potions from parts of dead toads. Rumors spread that she poisoned people. She managed to escape prosecution because she said she was pregnant.

In 1540, another cluster of trials was conducted in the Salazar Valley in the Pyrenees. The accused were purportedly supposed to have "reneged God and with filth and burnt toads and other poisons, they have used poisoned powders to kill." According to Balanza, their followers "have gathered many times, both day and night, in their gatherings and festivities and dances of the witches." Their acts were called "maleficia."

In 1560, Graciana Belca was accused of using herbal mixtures to control others. She was an elderly woman, but she was still tortured on the rack and given water tortures. She was sentenced to one hundred lashings and then exiled for ten years. Because she suffered broken arms and was maimed, it is doubtful she survived. However, there is no record of what happened to her.

In 1575, Abbot Pedro de Anocibar, who wasn't an official magistrate, reported to the Royal Commission that Maria Johan had taken two young boys to a witches' gathering. Johan indicated to the abbot that she had been troubled by evil spirits most of her life, but she herself wasn't a witch. Two other Basque villagers were also accused, including a man and a woman. Poor Maria was burned at the stake in Pamplona. One of her assistants did too, but the other escaped. Hysteria took root, and in the course of seven months, seventeen more trials were held. All of the sentences aren't known, but many were accused of manipulating toads, attending covens, and poisoning crops. Most of these people were exiled.

The stories became even more preposterous. It was reported that women in white were seen floating above a house but then changed into cats, dogs, or pigs.

In 1609, Pierre de Lancre, a French judge, held the opinion that the Basque people, in particular, had a predilection for witchcraft. Sentences were more severe on the French side of the Basque Country. Pierre de Lancre was called upon as an inquisitor to resolve a dispute between some people with the lord of Urtubi. Urtubi is a town in the Basque province of Labourd. The citizens accused the lord and his followers of being witches. It was said that Urtubi's followers would "dance indecently, ate excessively; make love diabolically; perform acts of atrocious sodomy; blaspheme scandalously." They would also keep toads, lizards, and vipers, and it was said they engaged in passionate love-making with goats.

Pierre de Lancre's witch hunt in Labourd resulted in the executions of seventy Basques. De Lancre wanted to continue, but he was dismissed from office.

According to Basque mythology, their chief goddess, Mari, had helpers called *sorginaks*. A *sorginak* became equated with a demon who assists the devil or his legions. Because of that, the Basques became a target for those who were inundated with the mass hysteria that swept through Europe.

In Spain, Alonso de Salazar Frías, a priest and a lawyer, was selected as an inquisitor for the tribunal of Logroño (La Rioja) in 1609. Accusations streamed in, and by 1610, around six people were burned at the stake.

Salazar toured the region, collecting more evidence. He pledged to pardon anyone who "confessed." When he returned, he claimed to have information on as many as 1,800 individuals. Most of those people retracted their statements later.

Jurisdictional and Moral Issues

There were issues surrounding the jurisdiction for the courts in which witchcraft cases were held. In Madrid, there was the Inquisition Tribunal, and in Navarre, there was the Royal Council. For years, there were disputes over which court had the right to hear and decide these cases. The Royal Council of Navarre argued that since inquisitors didn't have to be lawyers, it had the right to try cases. Navarrese courts further argued that the Inquisitional courts only imposed penalties like confession and penance. The Royal Council, however, was empowered to deal with the secular aspects of these crimes, like the destruction of property or bodily harm. Witnesses gave conflicting accounts of supernatural occurrences. Others brought up incidents related to crop damage. On a subjective level, accusers could use the court to rid themselves of bad neighbors or people inflicted with mental illness.

These trials usually focused upon whether or not people were *malas Christians* (bad Christians) or *buena Christians* (good Christians), as defined by the Catholic Church. Cases were also influenced by the beliefs of local villagers and the personalities of those accused.

In later medieval courts, torture was considered a legitimate way of securing the "truth." To lend validity to a sentence, it was believed that testimonies by two "unimpeachable" individuals were invaluable. That way, convictions could be obtained despite a paucity of circumstantial evidence.

In many cases, the Royal Council of Navarre transferred cases to the Spanish Inquisition Tribunal. Their Sentences were usually lighter, and there were restrictions about physical torture. Executions couldn't be ordered without approval from the king. So, when judges felt a person shouldn't be dealt with severely, the accused were sent to Spain. However, there was a problem with that. Sometimes, the Inquisitional courts would impose a sentence of imprisonment, but conditions were so bad in the prisons that people died, particularly the elderly.

Autonomy/Home Rule in the Southern Basque Country

In 1451, Labourd was made a French autonomous province. In 1589, Lower Navarre was incorporated into France with the accession of King Henry IV.

The Southern Basque Country refers to those provinces that lie geographically within Spain: Biscay, Gipuzkoa, Álava, and Upper Navarre. Throughout the 13th and 14th centuries, the Basques had their own government consisting of oral traditions and common law. They had general councils called foral parliaments, each of which covered a province. These parliaments had elected representatives from among the local inhabitants.

During the Middle Ages, the provinces were divided into Basques *señoríos* or *jaurerriak* ("Basque lordships"). They were hereditary land titles to territories that were run by a count or a lord. The kings of various Basque areas, like the king of Pamplona, had to swear allegiance to that leader.

The *Fueros* in Spain

The charters, or *fueros*, of the individual Basque districts gave the Basques a degree of fiscal independence, a court system, control of the military draft, and constitutional rights of non-Castilian provinces. Castilian kings had to swear to observe Basque laws.

Difficulties arose when there were conflicts between laws in the local territories and the central government. For example, a person might be able to escape conviction by fleeing from Aragon to a Basque autonomous province.

In 1719, when the more absolutist Spanish monarch Philip V attempted to centralize his power, the Basque provinces were able to maintain their autonomy because they supported Philip in the War of Spanish Succession.

End of Home Rule in France

The historic Basque provinces of Labourd, Soule, and Lower Navarre were geographically located in France. In 1733 and in 1748, the Estates-General—the governing body in France—suppressed self-government in the Basque provinces for the purposes of taxation and control of the central government.

Labourd had been weakened by an economic downturn. A Basque patriot from Labourd, Dominique-Joseph Garat, vigorously defended Labourd's democratic status. By 1790, the Estates-General morphed into the National Assembly, and it abolished home rule in the Basque Country. In 1791, a new constitution was passed in France, confirming that.

War of the Pyrenees

The formidable Pyrenees

Between 1793 and 1795, the War of the Pyrenees was fought between the Kingdom of France and the Kingdoms of Spain and Portugal. The War of the Pyrenees was one of the many French Revolutionary Wars. Initially, Spain remained neutral, but when France declared war on Spain, they entered the war. The French army then recruited Basques from the French Basque provinces; this was a practice that continued into the 19th century. The French army invaded the province of Labourd, and there were many deaths (1,600 in all) and mass deportations. Many of the affected people fled to America.

To make the chronology easier to follow, the two theaters of this war have been split into separate sections.

War in the Eastern Pyrenees

In April of 1793, Spanish Captain General Antonio Ricardos commanded the Catalonian army. He invaded the region of Cerdagne and captured the commune of Saint-Laurent-de-Cerdans. Following that, he boldly defeated the poorly trained French troops at the Tech River, located right on the Spanish-French border in the county of Roussillon. The French were commanded by an elderly commander, Mathieu Henri Marchant de La Houlière, who became so depressed by his failure to defend the area that he committed suicide. Spain then divided their army into two divisions: the Army of the Eastern Pyrenees and the Army of the Western Pyrenees.

In May, Ricardos attacked a French encampment under the command of Louis-Charles de Flers near Mas Deu. Once the French were gone from there, Ricardos struck Fort de Bellegarde at the town of Le Perthus. He promptly placed it under siege. About a month and a half later, the French gave up the fort.

It was now July. Ricardos pursued the French toward Perpignan, the capital city of Roussillon. Ricardos separated his army into five columns. In the beginning, they made good progress. The third column even captured some hills there. However, the second column, under Jerónimo Girón-Moctezuma, Marquis de las Amarillas, was delayed and failed to support the third column like he was supposed to. Louis-Charles de Flers then attacked the separated third column and forced it back. Another column turned around to help, and they were able to reform their position. But then the French attacked full-force. Unfortunately, the columns were too far apart, and the French defeated them.

During the following months, the war went both ways. At times, the French were able to repel the Spanish back, and at others, the Spanish were able to win some solid victories.

In December 1793, the Portuguese allied with Ricardos. This combined force won a victory in the Battle of Villelongue-dels-Monts. This was followed by the Battle of Collioure at the end of the month, which saw the Spanish winning the French ports of Collioure and Port-Vendres.

Ricardos went to Madrid to ask for reinforcements. The weather up in the mountains was cold and wet, and it took its toll on Ricardos, who was sixty-six years old. Ricardos died of pneumonia in March. His successor, Alejandro O'Reilly, died ten days later. Luis Firmin de Carvajal was then given command of the Army of Catalonia. The French also took on a new commander, Jacques François Dugommier.

In April of 1794, Dugommier returned to Boulou to expel the Spanish. He was successful, as he managed to force the Spanish to abandon their equipment. In May, the French recaptured the port of Collioure and took 7,000 Spanish from the garrison there as prisoners.

Dugommier then placed a siege upon the Spanish-held fort in Bellegarde. In August, the Spanish attempted to relieve the siege, but it was unsuccessful, and the starving soldiers were forced to surrender. Many had already starved to death.

In November of 1794, the Spanish troops were joined by the Portuguese. The French defeated them at the Battle of the Black

Mountain. It was a tough battle for both sides. Dugommier died early in the battle and was replaced by Dominique Catherine de Pérignon. Luis de Carvajal, who led the Spanish, also died. The Spanish/Portuguese suffered extreme losses, as estimates believe that 10,000 were killed or wounded, and 8,000 were captured. The French lost less, although it was still a great number; it is believed 3,000 were killed or wounded.

War in the Western Pyrenees

In February of 1794, the French under Commanders Jean Henri Guy Nicholas de Frégeville and Augustin Lespinasse were able to hold their hilltop positions and fortress during the Battle of Sans Culottes Camp against the Spanish cavalry and infantry under José Urrutia y de las Casas. Losses on both sides were small.

In March, the Spanish Basques were assigned to guard the borders of Sara, Itxassou, and Ascain against any incoming French troops. They didn't and instead fled back to the Basque Country. As a punishment, the residents of the Basque villages were herded into carts and taken to the Landes, a large wooded area in Gascony. Their valuables were taken, and it is believed that thousands were taken from their homes, with around 1,600 dying in the process.

In July, the French Army of the Western Pyrenees attacked the Spanish positions, which led to the Battle of the Baztan Valley. The commander of the French army, Bon-Adrien Jeannot de Moncey, led his forces to a decisive victory over the Spanish. The French proceeded along the Bidasoa River and snatched the town of Hondarribia.

The following month, the city of San Sebastián in Gipuzkoa surrendered to the French. The nobles of San Sebastián attempted to negotiate with the French. They claimed they supported the French revolutionary ideals and made a petition to be joined to France. However, they had caveats to that proposal; they wanted French respect for their regional laws, the freedom to practice Catholicism, and a set of rules for the management of war-related issues. The

French refused to accept the conditions, and the Gipuzkoa representatives were imprisoned or exiled. When General Moncey heard this, he came out in support of the governmental institutions of Gipuzkoa, which enraged the authorities in Madrid. As a result, the Spanish lashed out at the Basque residents living in Gipuzkoa. When the representatives were released from their imprisonment (those that survived at least), they were accused of high treason by Spanish authorities and placed on trial.

In October, Moncey moved into Navarre, and the French proved victorious in the Battle of Orbaitzeta. The Spanish then gave up their territory north of Pamplona, and they also lost their arms foundry at Eugi and Orbaitzeta.

Winter was setting in, and Moncey headed home. The winter was harsh, and Moncey lost many men to disease and the cold. The following year, the French came back in full force. In July 1795, both Vitoria and Bilbao fell to the French, ending the war and leading to the Peace of Basel.

The Peace of Basel

Manuel Godoy, First Secretary of State of Spain, was concerned that the province of Gipuzkoa would try to cede to France, as they had wished to do at the beginning of the war. In exchange for Gipuzkoa, Godoy gave up two-thirds of the Caribbean island of Hispaniola to France. Upon the request of French commander Moncey, amendments were added to the agreement, stating that Spain would make no reprisals against those Basques who had expressed allegiance to France. This treaty was signed in 1795.

The Ineffective Bayonne Statute

In 1804, Napoleon Bonaparte crowned himself emperor of France. In 1808, Napoleon invaded and conquered Spain. He named his brother, Joseph, as the new king of Spain. The Bayonne Statute was negotiated with Joseph Bonaparte. This statute specifically had wording in it that recognized the Basque principality, allowing for a degree of home rule. This statute was virtually ignored in practice.

In 1812, the Spanish Constitution, also known as the Constitution of Cádiz, was passed. However, the Constitution of Cádiz totally overlooked the Basque Country altogether. It specified that Spain was a nation in its own right. Because no allowances were made recognizing the *fueros*—the charters—of the Basque districts, the Basque population was concerned they would lose any chance of having a self-government. As a result, deputies were sent to Cádiz in order to clear this up. They called upon the Parliament of Navarre to make this change. However, their plea was turned down.

At the heart of the Basque issue was the overlapping Peninsular War, which was fought between Britain, Portugal, and France over the leadership of Spain. In 1814, after that war, Joseph Bonaparte abdicated the throne of Spain, and power was restored to the former monarch, Ferdinand VII. King Ferdinand was an absolute monarch. With the ascendancy of Ferdinand, a return to orthodoxy took place. Catholicism was the mandatory religion in Spain and in the Basque Country.

The three provinces where the Basque regions lay in France—Labourd, Soule, and Lower Navarre—were under French jurisdiction. The Basques who lived there were recruited into the armed forces of France. This area is what is called the French Basque Country today.

Chapter 7 – The Modern Period

The First Carlist War in Spain, 1833-1840

In 1833, Queen Isabella II took the throne, but she wasn't even three years old. Don Carlos María Isidro Benito de Borbón was the younger son of Charles IV and became a pretender to the throne under the name of Charles V. He was more traditional and supported the cause of Basque autonomy.

The Basque supporters of Don Carlos rallied under the military leadership of Basque Tomás de Zumalacárregui, and an army was formed, which was financed by the Basque provinces in Spain. Carlism, named after Don Carlos, which was essentially a Spanish political movement, supported Don Carlos as the legitimate heir to the Spanish throne as opposed to Isabella II. It eventually morphed into an ideological conflict between conservatives and liberals in the Basque provinces. The Basques became alarmed, as they thought they would never regain home rule they had once achieved through the *fueros*, which had been abolished by the former Spanish Constitution.

The Spanish Basques decided to join the army that represented the traditionalists. They were concerned that a more liberal stance would further threaten their rights to rule themselves, as it wouldn't help their cause for maintaining some level of self-government.

The Basque Motivations

The Basques were highly skilled masters of the sea in the areas of northern Spain and southwestern France. The Basques had numerous ports and established trade routes, and the late King Ferdinand VII of Spain had been pleased with that arrangement. However, the Constitution of Cádiz eliminated home rule and the *fueros*. The Basques were promised that Charles, the contender to the throne, would protect their individual freedoms and reestablish the *fueros*. However, this war pitted Basque against Basque, as not all the Basques believed in Don Carlos, although the vast majority did.

In 1834, Zumalacárregui and the Basques descended from the mountains into Álava and defeated General Manuel O'Doyle. By 1835, nearly all of Gipuzkoa and Biscay were in Carlist hands.

Zumalacárregui eventually started to rely upon supplies confiscated from the enemy and was forced into fighting a guerilla war. The Carlists wanted to gain control of the seaports, but Zumalacárregui preferred to march to Madrid and claim the throne for Don Carlos. Zumalacárregui obeyed his orders, though, and besieged Bilbao in 1835. He was wounded there, and due to some poor medical attention, he died. Subsequent clashes turned against the Carlists. Some of the contemporary supporters of Basque governance, like John Francis Bacon, didn't trust Carlos to keep his agreement to establish home rule, saying that Carlos "would quickly find excuses for infringing them."

In 1839, the Convention of Vergara, also known as the "Embrace of Vergara," ended the First Carlist War. By virtue of that treaty, Basque home rule was modified, along with the *fueros*. A follow-up act, the Compromise Act of 1841, dissolved the Kingdom of Navarre, making it a Spanish province. However, Navarre retained its control over taxation within its province.

Economic Consequences

After the First Carlist War, General Espartero became the regent for young Isabella II. As a result of the war, the treasury was depleted. Trade, which had greatly benefited Pamplona, fell dramatically because the trade between Pamplona and Bayonne had all but ceased once the customs were moved by the French government in the French Basque provinces. Also, some common lands were confiscated by the French government, leaving many French Basques poverty-stricken. Famines occurred, and there was a massive emigration to the United States by the French Basques.

The Third Carlist War, 1872–1876

Although there was a Second Carlist War in Spain, it didn't affect the Basques that much. The Third Carlist War, however, was crucial for the Basque Country. The Spanish government was unstable, having gone through a high turnover of government officials, and the poor economic situation in the country contributed to the discontent of the Spanish people. Back in 1868, Queen Isabella II abdicated the throne and was succeeded by an Italian prince, Amadeo I, rather than a Spaniard, which gave rise to popular resentment.

The Carlists supported Carlos VII, the new pretender to the throne, and recruited the Basques to rise up against the Spanish government in 1872. The Basques established a temporary state of their own in the Spanish provinces of Álava, Biscay, Gipuzkoa, and Navarre. They demanded the restoration of home rule and charters, like the *fueros* of the past. The Basques also wanted an exemption from the Spanish military draft, as they did not wish to fight in their wars.

Despite the fact they weren't well-equipped, the Basques occupied some Spanish towns, including Estella and La Seu d'Urgell in Navarre, and laid siege to the cities of San Sebastián and Bilbao. The Carlists then set up the town of Estella as their new temporary capital.

The First Spanish Republic, 1873-1874

Unfortunately, the Basques weren't successful with their sieges of San Sebastián or Bilbao, but they did gain the attention of both France and Spain to their cause. In 1873, Amadeo I abdicated, and Spain set up the First Spanish Republic until they could resolve the succession crisis. In December of the following year, Alfonso XII, the son of Queen Isabella II, was made the king of Spain.

Although the monarchy was reestablished, the Carlists continued fighting. Many Carlists either flocked to the other side or were put on trial, so the remaining Carlists mostly tried to hold on to the positions they had after this point. The Carlist general Torcuato Mendiri was able to score a victory at Lácar, and he was also able to capture military equipment from the government troops and take hundreds of prisoners. About a thousand men died in this battle, mostly those from the government forces. Sadly, Mendiri wasn't able to repeat his victory in 1875, and he was forced to retreat from the government forces. Following that, he was dismissed. His replacement, Prince Alfonso, Count of Caserta, wasn't able to stop the government's advance, despite the fact he had a lot of equipment and men at his disposal.

By 1876, the Carlists were losing ground and had to surrender the town of Estella. Once Estella was lost, the Carlists lost heart and fled. Even Carlos VII, the pretender, left Spain altogether. In February of 1876, King Alfonso XII marched into the Basque city of Pamplona in triumph.

After the Third Carlist War, the Basque provinces lost their home rule and were placed under martial law. The Spanish government then entered into negotiations with the Basques for what came to be called the Basque Economic Agreement.

Basque Economic Agreement

Because of the unique needs of the Basque people, an economic agreement was reached with Spain in 1878 related to taxation. This agreement stated that the Basque provinces were "to pay taxes according to their means, in the same way as other Spaniards." However, the Spanish government did present a certain quota they expected based on past performance. The *fueros* of the past were abolished, but provincial councils were allowed to continue as before, which would develop their own system for the collection of taxes.

Besides the taxes placed on individuals, there were set taxes, such as territorial taxes (property), industrial taxes (for example, on the production of iron), taxes on the transfer of money, a stamp tax, and a consumption tax.

Rise of Basque Nationalism in the 19th Century

The Basques in France became politically polarized between the Royalists and the Republicans. Most of the Basques were Royalists, which was a party that was identified with Catholicism. After the War of the Pyrenees, French was considered the national language. As time went on, the Basques began to speak their own language in the Basque communities.

The Basques in France became more involved in the economy when the railway through Aquitaine was completed in 1864. The mingling of Basque and non-Basque peoples took place, and tourism even arrived.

Even though the Basques in the Spanish areas fared somewhat better than the French after the Carlist Wars, the Spanish never really appreciated the uniqueness of the Basque cultures or practices as they once had when the *fueros* were in place. Although no one could really annihilate the use of the Basque language, especially in the Basque provinces, they tried.

In the Spanish Parliament, Sabino Arana created the Basque Nationalist Party in 1895. Initially, the Basque Nationalists were somewhat xenophobic. De Arana was a purist and believed that the Basque race was morally superior and likewise supported anti-liberal Catholicism. He believed all members should be able to prove

Basque ancestry. He discouraged the immigration of non-Basque Spaniards and strongly encouraged Basques to marry only within the Basque community and to speak the Basque language.

Chapter 8 – Economy

Expert Seaman

The Basques have been and still are excellent seamen, fishermen, and shipbuilders. The well-known French explorer Samuel de Champlain once said the Basques were "the cleverest men at this fishing." He was specifically referring to their whaling skills.

The Basques had a wide coastline that opened out to the Bay of Biscay and used their ports on the northern coast to sail tow Ireland and northern England, where they conducted a hefty trade. Whale oil was used in lamps in the early days; whale blubber could be used to manufacture soap, cosmetics, and in the manufacturing of leather.

Local Whaling

Whaling in the 18th century; it was treacherous but lucrative.

Whaling was more common among the Basques in Spain, especially in the ports of Gipuzkoa and the Biscay provinces, than in France. King Sancho VI, also known as Sancho the Wise, who served as the king of Navarre in the 12th century, had created a successful whaling industry for the Basques. Whaling fared quite well until the end of the 19th century. Sancho VI granted certain privileges to the town of San Sebastián, allowing the people there to distribute and house whaling products. He also had his seamen concentrate on the city of Bayonne, where they had a brisk market. Duties had to be paid on the storage of these products, which increased cash flow.

Of course, whaling is discouraged today, but at that time, there were sufficient whales in the area, so it had no significant impact until later centuries when overexploitation diminished the whale population off the Bay of Biscay and in the North Atlantic fishing areas.

North Atlantic Fishing

Whaling accelerated off the coast of England and continued to be lucrative through the years. This was beneficial for both the Basques and the English, who, in turn, prepared the whale products and shipped them overseas, sending them as far as Brazil. In Brazil, Basque whalers instructed the Brazilians in the trade and in the development of new uses for whale blubber (for instance, whale blubber could be used as lubrication for their machinery in the sugar mills). The Brazil trade came to a screeching halt when some Basque sailors cut down trees for brazilwood. Brazilwood is extremely useful in making masts for ships. Portugal, which controlled the colony of Brazil, was incensed, as they had a royal monopoly on the product.

Through the years, the Basque whaling industry ran head-first into difficulties with foreign interests, such as Iceland and northern Norway. Those countries resented infringement by Basque whalers, as whaling was a part of their history as well. The Basques were able to conduct business for a while, but they eventually had to abandon those waters after foreigners destroyed some of their gear in retribution for the incursions. Piracy and plundering sometimes took place at sea when English ships attacked them. Even Danish ships seized barrels of blubber when the Basques came into port to sell them. Human interference started to become even more dangerous than the actual process of whaling.

Industrial Expansion

The Basques lost a lot of advantages after the suppression of the *fueros* following the Carlist Wars. The Biscay area used to produce high-quality iron, which they sold locally, but in the 19th century, they began exporting the ore to Great Britain, which was more profitable. The entrepreneurial Basques reinvested it in developing equipment and machinery to develop more advanced iron and steel products for export. This touched off a "mini-industrial boom."

To keep up with demand, foreigners were hired. Most spoke Spanish, but they had different cultures than the Basques. In addition, these newcomers weren't investors. They were very poor and looking for any steady job they could find.

The railway system that had recently been put in place was excellent for shipping products to other areas of the Basque Country and to ports for overseas shipping. The railroad also helped develop the coastal areas, where resorts were built for tourists. Since the Basques had many buildings there with Romanesque architecture, sightseeing often occurred.

Mining

In the 19th century, Biscay's industries expanded exponentially. One of the earliest iron factories was called Santa Ana de Bolueta. The population of the area nearly doubled, as the Basque people migrated there for work. Another city named Barakaldo grew quickly as well. This city had a dynamite factory to service the mines, and that, in turn, triggered the erection of a steelwork plant. The Basques hired other Basques from the inland areas, but there weren't enough workers, as the Basques had lost so many of their people to emigration. As a result, they had to depend upon immigrant labor. By the latter part of the 19th century, the humble province of Biscay was the world's leading exporter of iron ore.

The quality of their ore was quite high, and during that era, foreign investors took a keen interest in the Basque iron mines. Britain was its largest client. In 1902, Altos Hornos de Vizcaya was established. It was the merger of three businesses: Altos Hornos de Bilbao, La Vizcaya, and La Iberia. Over ninety million tons of ore were extracted at its peak level of production.

Most of the mines were in the hands of the Basque elite and wealthy. In fact, just a small number of clan families—namely, the Chavarri and Ibarra—owned half of the mining interests. Their mines produced over 60 percent of the iron in Spain. Unfortunately, this forced smaller companies to go out of business.

The Basques needed the coal produced in the province of Asturias to the west to fuel their iron industry, but the Asturians had to depend upon unreliable and expensive rail services to transport it to Biscay. So, the Basques had to get coal from the British, who sold it cheaper. Thus, foreigners didn't invest in the coal mines, as they made less profit from them. Spain also charged very high tariffs for its exports, which caused a decline in orders. It was only during the First World War that the Basques and the Asturians were able to turn a profit. After the war, however, the coal and iron industries went into a crisis.

In Gipuzkoa province, the textile industries flourished. There were textile companies such as Algodonera de San Antonio and paper factories in Oria and Tolosa. By 1920, there were more fabric companies and a small sewing machine company, which was simply called Alfa.

Chapter 9 – The Twentieth Century

Basque Nationalism

After the Carlist Wars of the 19th century, there was an emigration of Basques to the Americas. To keep up with demands for trade, foreigners came into the Basque Country. However, the Basques desperately wanted to preserve their unique culture and language, and the Basques felt that these immigrants were threatening the integrity of their culture and language. In 1931, the Basque Nationalist Party and the Republicans worked together to develop the Statute of Estella, which called for the creation of an autonomous state for the Spanish Basque counties of Álava, Biscay, and Gipuzkoa. It didn't receive enough support because of divisions among the Carlists. A more abridged version was proposed, but political events interceded, thus delaying any action.

The Second Spanish Republic, 1931–1939

The initiation of the Second Spanish Republic in 1931 brought about an ambivalent reaction from the Basques. The provinces of Biscay, Gipuzkoa, and, to a limited extent, Álava supported the Republicans. Even though the leftist Republicans maintained an anti-Catholic policy, they did support a degree of autonomy for the

Basques. Navarre, though, was opposed to the new republic. They had legal difficulties regarding the validity of the voting process and arguments about the nomenclature used to identify it.

The Short-Lived Statute of Autonomy of the Basque Country of 1936

In 1936, the leading political faction, the Republicans, achieved the long-desired passage of the Statute of Autonomy of the Basque Country. It protected the traditional privileges granted to the Basques from the past. José Antonio Aguirre took over leadership of the state of "Euskadi," becoming the first president of the Basque Country. His first act was to muster forces to go up against the rival faction in the ongoing Spanish Civil War. Aguirre formed a conciliatory government composed of socialists, communists, Republicans, and Nationalists.

The Spanish Civil War, 1936–1939

This war pitted a myriad of organizations fighting for the control of Spain and the kind of government Spain would embrace. One side, generally called the Republicans, represented groups that even espoused conflicting ideologies. Despite their differences, they adamantly opposed the other side, called the Nationalists. The Basques were aligned with the Republicans.

Manuel Azaña was the leader of the Republicans. This side also had the support of the regular Spanish army, called Ejército Popular de la República ("People's Army of the Republic). There were many other groups as well, each with its own agenda:

> 1. The Popular Front – included socialists, communists, Valencian nationalists, and others. The Valencian nationalists supported a separate national state for the people of the Catalonia region.

> 2. The UGT (*Unión General de Trabajadores*, or General Union of Workers) – a Spanish labor union.

3. The CNT-FAI (*Confederación Nacional del Trabajo,* or National Confederation of Labour/*Federación Anarquista Ibérica,* or Iberian Anarchist Federation) –anarchist organizations that were closely linked.

4. The *Generalitat de Catalunya,* or Government of Catalonia – the self-government of Catalonia in northeastern Spain.

5. *Euzko Gudarostea* – the Basque army.

6. International Brigades – military units supported by the communists.

The Nationalists were led by General Francisco Franco. Franco sought to return Spain back into the embrace of the monarchy, preferably with him as the leader.

Francisco Franco

The Nationalist groups are listed below:

1. The *FET y de las JONS* (*Falange Española Tradicionalista y de las Juntas de Ofensiva Nacional Sindicalista,* or Traditionalist Spanish Phalanx and that of the

Councils of the National Syndicalist Offensive) – a party that supported the former Carlists and the candidacy of Francisco Franco.

2. The *FE de las JONS* (*Falange Española de las Juntas de Ofensiva Nacional Sindicalista*, or Spanish Phalanx of the National Syndicalist Offensive) – the Fascists; in 1936, it combined with the *FET y de las JONS* to become the only legal party of Spain.

3. The Requetés – a group that supported a splinter faction of the former Carlists.

4. The *Renovación Española*, or Spanish Renovation – Royalists who supported the restoration of the former monarch.

5. The Army of Africa – specifically Morocco, which was a Spanish colony at the time.

6. Italy – Italy, which was ruled by Fascists, supported Franco.

7. Germany – Germany, led by Adolf Hitler, supported Franco and his Nationalist Party to create support for himself and his future plans.

Francisco Franco of the Nationalists had his sights on capturing Madrid and destroying the Second Spanish Republic. However, before moving to Madrid, he decided to attempt to gain possession of the province of Biscay, along with all of its ports along the Bay of Biscay.

The Bombing of Guernica

Franco was very much opposed to the Basques and what they stood for. On April 26th, 1937, his German supporters sent out the *Luftwaffe*'s Condor Legion—the Nazi German air force that assisted in the Spanish Civil War—which heavily bombed the town of Guernica in Biscay. There were five waves of bombings, and the aircraft carried between 100 and 110 pounds of bombs. Three-quarters of the town was destroyed. Roads leading in and out of the city center were blown apart. Oddly enough, the arms factory wasn't destroyed, nor was the *Gernikako Arbola* ("The Tree of Gernika"), the oak tree that symbolized the Basque civilization. There are varying estimates of the death toll from this attack. Eyewitnesses at the time believe there were about 1,700 casualties.

Tree of Gernika

Battle of Bilbao

Aguirre's government only held power until June of 1937, which was when the Nationalists attacked Bilbao. An "iron ring" was built to protect the government. This was a ring of hastily constructed fortifications around the capital city. The ring was easily breached during the Battle of Bilbao. With the fall of Bilbao, Aguirre and the government moved to Trucios, Catalonia, and Santander successively. The Republican army went to Santander to negotiate a deal, but Franco canceled any agreement and imprisoned 22,000 of them.

Some were freed, but others remained in prison. Five hundred seventy men were executed.

In August to September of 1937, the campaign moved to the province of Aragon. The Republicans, under Commander Enrique Lister, had a huge infantry force backed up by tanks and aircraft. The Nationalists depended exclusively on infantry, but they had a huge number of men. This campaign was a Republican victory, but they failed to gain significant ground.

The Republicans still had a significant amount of territory in Cantabria, so they moved their offensive there. Unfortunately for the Republicans, the Nationalists had nearly doubled the number of forces.

The Republicans launched two attacks against the Nationalists, but both attempts failed, which led to the Basques losing control of Bilboa. The barbarity of this attack was memorialized by the famous painter Pablo Picasso in his work, *Guernica*.

The End before the End

With the help of the masterful Basque sailors, the Republicans secured control of a number of coastal cities. However, Franco's forces overran the Republican forces in mainland Spain, and it didn't help that Madrid was placed under siege in November of 1936. The Republicans were able to stave off the Nationalists for quite some time.

The "Santoña Treason"

After enduring that savage attack, the Basques surrendered, doing so before the Spanish Civil War was over. The Italian forces represented Franco, and they signed the Santoña Agreement, in which the Basque army would surrender. Following that, the captured Basque soldiers would be treated as prisoners of war according to international law.

When Franco saw the agreement, he trashed it and imprisoned 22,000 captured Basque soldiers. Three hundred were freed several months later, but 510 were executed. The rest remained in prison for an unspecified period of time. Hence, the Santoña Agreement was dubbed the "Santoña Treason."

In 1938, the Nationalists drove through the Republican forces, cutting them in two. Franco then turned to Catalonia and captured Barcelona, which was its capital. Seeing that they were losing, the Republicans offered to make a settlement. Franco refused their overture and kept on fighting.

Door-to-door fighting during the Spanish Civil War

The Battle of Madrid

The Republicans knew they had the advantage when it came to Madrid, but Nationalist Emilio Mola wasn't going to let that stop him. On November 8th, 1936, he attacked Madrid. German Panzer I tanks came thundering in, while bombs from the German Condor Legion dropped from the sky. Republican forces fought back with their rifles and a rationed amount of ammunition. They knew they were outmatched, and some tried to flee, but Republican General José Miaja prevented them, saying they should die rather than run like cowards.

A modest relief force arrived to support the Nationalists, but they were poorly trained. Their lack of skill gave the Republicans a boost of confidence. On November 9th, a Republican force attacked the Nationalists at the Casa de Campo and forced them back.

On November 12th, a Republican force arrived to help. They attacked Cerro de los Ángeles Hill in order to prevent the Nationalists from cutting off routes to southern Spain. The confusion of languages confounded that effort, but luckily, the road to Valencia in southern Spain was accessible.

On November 19th, the Nationalists attacked the University City quarter in the heart of Madrid. Door-to-door fighting ensued. Counterattacks from the Republicans occurred throughout this district, as they were not willing to go without a fight. Franco realized he was losing a lot of his infantry due to the relentless attacks of the Republicans, and he made the hard decision of pulling them out so he could try and mitigate his losses.

Since the ground invasion did not work, Franco turned to aerial bombardment. It is hard to say if this invasion was worth it. The causalities were rather low, and people around the world condemned the action since it was one of the first bombings of civilians in history.

The fighting continued. At times, both sides would be so worn out that the fighting would briefly stop, but no one was taking a definitive lead. However, this changed in early 1939. By that point, only Madrid and a few other strongholds were left under Republican control. Madrid fell in late March, and Valencia, the last major holdout, surrendered soon after. Francisco Franco entered Madrid and declared victory on April 1st, 1939.

Atrocities

There were mass atrocities committed during this war, as there were so many smaller factions who had their own ideological differences.

Within the first few months, 7,000 priests, monks, and nuns were executed by the Nationalists. Nationalist fighters raped Republican women. During 1940, 500,000 people were sent to concentration camps. Many of those were Spanish refugees hoping to find refuge in France, but as soon as they arrived, they were sent to concentration camps. The estimates of people executed after the war numbered 250,000.

The Republicans were also guilty of committing atrocities. Most notably, the Republicans targeted clergy and those civilians they believed to be Nationalist sympathizers. The number of how many people actually died is hard to estimate, as Franco's regime inflated the numbers for propaganda purposes, but it is believed to be around 50,000.

It is estimated that up to a million people were killed in the Spanish Civil War. It was the bloodiest and most brutal in Spanish history.

The French Basques during World War II

Just a year after the Spanish Civil War ended, the French Basque Country was occupied by the German military. The French government moved from Paris to Vichy, setting up in what was called the Free Zone. Areas within the small province of Soule and the eastern areas of Lower Navarre in France were within this zone. The Basques were supportive of the Vichy regime. Philippe Pétain was Chief of State of Vichy France.

Vichy France, although it was essentially a Nazi client state, conducted secret operations to resist the German occupation, which was, at the time, enmeshed in World War II. Northern France, including the French Basque Country, was under German control until the end of the war. Any Spanish Basques who may have fled Spain were immediately thrown into concentration camps.

Basque Code-Talkers

Because *Euskara*, the Basque language, was so different from the Indo-European languages, some Basques living in the United States, China, and the Philippines were used as "code-talkers." A code-talker is someone who speaks an uncommon language. These code-talkers helped the Allied war effort by transmitting secret messages to American troops operating in the Pacific theater. It was said that Lieutenants Nemesio Aguirre and Fernández Bakaicoa sent a couple of messages about the Battle of Guadalcanal. There was a desire to hire more Basque code-talkers, but there weren't enough of them living within a free country to recruit. So, Native Americans were mostly employed for that duty.

Francisco Franco

Francisco Franco became the president of Spain after the Spanish Civil War. He discussed the possibility of getting involved with Adolf Hitler and the Nazi regime in World War II, but the concessions he wanted didn't appeal to Hitler. Franco also realized his military limitations, especially if his navy had to go up against that of Great Britain. He was once thanked by Winston Churchill for not blocking entry to the Allies at Gibraltar: "In the dark days of the war the attitude of the Spanish government in not giving our enemies passage through Spain was extremely helpful to us." In reality, Franco knew he couldn't block the passage at Gibraltar militarily, nor resist the Allies from getting some occasional help from him, such as aiding American pilots who had to bail out over Spain. However, Franco did give some aid to Hitler. For example, he permitted the Spanish to voluntarily join the Axis forces if they so wished.

He executed his political foes or put them into labor camps under inhumane conditions. Historians estimate that between 30,000 to 50,000 died due to his oppression.

Franco's Campaign against the Basques

Franco outlawed the Basque Nationalists, calling them communists, and banned the use of the Basque language. Franco was a fervent anti-communist, and he attempted to associate the Basques with communists to give himself an excuse to imprison them. Resistance associations formed, which were created out of the Basque political parties: the EAJ-PNV (Basque National Party—the acronym stands for the Spanish and the French spelling of the party), the Basque Nationalist Action, the Basque division of the Spanish Socialist Party, and the Basque Republican Left. Whenever any of those groups tried to schedule an activity, Franco had them arrested. Because of his fondness for imprisonment and executions, the Basque Nationalists went underground.

In 1951, about 250,000 workers in Álava and Navarre went on strike. Franco responded swiftly with beatings, dismissals from their jobs, and imprisonments. The EAJ-PNV, though, undertook other activities, such as holding Basque music festivals, art shows, and the narration of old folktales related to their culture. In hiding, they taught *Euskara*, the Basque language, to their children.

There were terrorist attacks during Franco's term of office that were sponsored by the underground organization ETA, which stands for *Euskadi Ta Askatasuna* ("Basque Homeland and Liberty"). It was a far-left organization, and its stated goal was total independence for all the Basque provinces in both Spain and France. ETA members even assassinated a contender for the next presidency, Luis Carrero Blanco, who held the same political views as Franco. In addition, ETA carried out other violent terrorist attacks.

During his rule, Franco employed GAL, which were death squads, to put a halt to any forms of terrorism. He also assigned GAL the task of killing any people he considered threats to his administration. That included ETA.

The first ETA member to be killed in action was Txabi Etxebarrieta in 1968. He was killed by the Civil Guard (Spain's oldest law enforcement agency), and his funeral attracted many people. Etxebarrieta's death was compared to that of Jesus Christ, and it was said that he died for the sake of the "religion" of the oppressed motherland. A well-known Basque sculptor, Jorge Oteiza, designed a Pietá-type figure in the church where Etxebarrieta was buried. He is considered to be a Basque patriot today.

Transition to Democracy

Francisco Franco stepped down in 1975, and Juan Carlos I became the king of Spain. Although Carlos told Franco he would continue his policies, he had no intention of doing so. He had witnessed the extreme repression of Franco and its sad aftermath. Although Franco had brought prosperity to the country, Carlos was saddened by the brutality of Franco's reign. There would, no doubt, be repercussions from that.

The Spanish Constitution of 1978 was passed, granting democratic reforms, including the suitable representation of the various provinces within the country. It was not a constitution in the strict sense, as observed by most other countries. It was deliberately open-ended. Spain is decentralized in the sense that it has different autonomous communities within its fifty provinces, each with its own specific laws. However, they had to answer to a higher power, which was the king and the overall administration of Spain.

According to Article 151 of the Spanish Constitution, the Statute of Autonomy of the Basque Country was passed in 1979. Each Basque community had its own constitution, which was voted upon by a three-quarters majority of each province. Each province had its own parliament, a legislative assembly, a council with an elected president and advisors (who were also elected by the assembly), and its own court of justice. They were allowed to levy and collect taxes, but the Basques had to contribute to the Spanish government for national defense, foreign affairs, maintenance of airports and public facilities for international commerce and travel, and ports.

This statute guaranteed liberties for the people of the provinces of Gipuzkoa, Álava, and Biscay. It put into place a parliamentary government with representatives elected by the Basque people. This statute also established universal suffrage and granted the Basques power to regulate industries, agriculture, tax collection, policing, and transportation. *Euskara*, the Basque language, was now permissible, along with Spanish.

Navarre chose to set up a chartered community, which is similar to an autonomous community. It controlled functions similar to that of the other three Basque provinces, although their political parties reflect a slight deviation, as there were pro-Basque parties and pro-Spanish parties. The pro-Basque parties heavily outnumber those of Spanish origin to this day. There is a movement inside Navarre to merge the province into the same autonomous status shared by the other three Basque provinces. Both the Basque language and Spanish is spoken in Navarre today.

Chapter 10 – Basque Terrorism

The Basque Nationalist Movement had to go underground during Franco's administration. During that time, they kept their movement alive and espoused total freedom for the Basque regions in Spain and France. At the heart of the Basque Nationalist Movement was the group ETA, whose name means "Basque Homeland and Liberty."

The introduction of democratic reforms and the Statute of Autonomy of the Basque Country appended to the Spanish Constitution fell short of ETA's goals for independence. From 1978 and onward, they staged a continual string of terrorist attacks.

There were thirteen fatal attacks during that period of time. For example, in May of 1978, a bomb exploded on a street in Pamplona, killing a Civil Guard in his passing vehicle. In September of 1978, two Civil Guards were killed by ETA gunmen; in May of 1980, three National Police officers were shot by ETA gunmen in the town of San Sebastián; in November of 1980, five people were killed, which included Civil Guards and a civilian; and in May of 1981, three Spanish military men were killed, and a bomb exploded in a Spanish destroyer. ETA was financed initially through robberies but later on through extortion.

ETA initiated a new group in the French Basque Country, the Iparretarrak ("the Northerners"). It was more of an anarchist group. Another group, the Comandos Autónomos Anticapitalistas ("Autonomous Anticapitalist Commandos"), also started carrying out terrorist attacks.

Failed Coup D'état

In 1981, when the country was in the process of electing Leopoldo Calvo-Sotelo as the new president, the Civil Guard and members of the army marched into the meeting room of the Congress of Deputies, with guns drawn. The coup failed, and Calvo-Sotelo was elected, but a three-way split in the political parties made it impossible for him to get sufficient support in the legislature. New elections were called for in 1982, and this time, Felipe González Márquez was elected.

Newly formed GAL were formed, even though they were illegal. These death squads murdered twenty-seven people. More were most likely killed, but those are the confirmed killings linked to them. Many injuries were also recorded as the result of bomb attacks. They targeted ETA members primarily and those of other leftist terrorist organizations. GAL performed these illegal executions from 1983 to 1987. This period was dubbed "Spain's dirty war." The people responsible for these killings were brought to court. Trials against them were initiated and continued for many years. To this day, people are still trying to discover what actually happened during "Spain's dirty war."

During that time, the Spanish government and ETA held negotiations, with occasional ceasefires being in effect. ETA members often hid on the French side of the border, where they trained and purchased arms. In 1987, France decided to no longer turn a blind eye to ETA activities, as they had done before, and extradited ETA militants back to Spain for prosecution. Basic militant operations in ETA was then passed into the hands of ETA youth groups, which instigated attacks in urban settings using guerilla tactics.

ETA terrorists were arrested and imprisoned in Spain. Some of the attacks subsided, and ETA again attempted to negotiate. Because of the gravity of the situation, the Spanish government refused to negotiate and considered them a criminal organization.

The Murder of Miguel Ángel Blanco

In 1997, a young Basque politician and councilor named Miguel Ángel Blanco was kidnapped by ETA. They indicated he would be released if ETA prisoners held in Spain were transferred to Basque prisons. The government refused, and Blanco was shot, after which he was dragged into the streets of San Sebastián. Blanco died in the hospital the next day on July 13th. Blanco was only twenty-five years old, and he was heralded as a hero to the cause of the People's Party, whose platform promotes democracy. His funeral was elaborate and very public. Not only was the government furious, but even some members of ETA and other militant organizations spoke out about the murder, condemning it. The Basque flag, called the *ikurrina*, was carried by the funeral train.

Memorial to Miguel Ángel Blanco

ETA held off their terror attacks during the 1998 Basque elections. The Basque Nationalists and the recently formed Euskal Herritarrok candidates won many seats, mostly due to the fact that the terrorist attacks had been suspended.

ETA Resumes Attacks

ETA resumed its terrorist attacks in 2000 (it should be noted ETA youth groups continued to promote the cause of nationalism throughout the years). In 2000, there were nearly fifty attacks on military, police, officials, politicians, journalists, and Basque companies. Not all the attacks took place in the Basque Country; many took place in Spain itself, especially Madrid. There were almost as many attacks the following year. These often did not involve gunfire, but many included bombs.

In 2002, Spain passed a law banning any organization that either directly or indirectly condoned violence as a means of forwarding its agenda. Newspapers that fostered violence were also banned.

Perhaps a Savior on the Rise

In 2004, José Luis Rodríguez Zapatero was elected as the new president of Spain. He held peace talks with ETA and the Basque and Spanish governments. A ceasefire was declared, but it was quickly broken by ETA, and attacks resumed all around Spain. In less than a year, four of their main leaders were arrested and imprisoned. By 2008, the government then banned some political parties they felt promoted or instigated violence, such as the Basque Nationalist Action, the youth groups, the Abertzale leftists, the Communist Party of the Basque Homelands, and others.

In 2011, the issue was brought to the international stage when citizens' groups from the Basque Country organized a meeting with leaders of other nations, including those who had dealt with similar issues. Among the attendees was Kofi Annan of the United Nations; Gro Harlem Brundtland, former Prime Minister of Norway; Bertie Ahearn, former Prime Minister of Ireland; Pierre Joxe, former interior minister of France; Gerry Adams, President of Sinn Féin; and Johnathan Powell, former Chief of Staff in England. Gerry Adams, for one, advocated that the Spanish government open a dialogue with ETA rather than refusing to talk to them. Bertie Ahearn of Ireland received a peace award in the Basque Country for his role in the conference. After the efforts of this international group, ETA declared "definitive cessation of its armed activity."

France then contacted Spain and apprised them of the fact that these activities hadn't ceased in the French Basque Country. There were still a number of weapons and ammunition caches on the French side of the border. The French hired some non-governmental groups to go into the Nationalists' dens and storage facilities. ETA members in France gave them the locations of their stashes, which were then confiscated by French and Spanish authorities.

As popular pressure against ETA increased and financial support waned, membership fell off dramatically. Most Basques who favored secession wanted to approach the issue with non-violence.

Finally, on May 3rd, 2018, ETA declared an end to their terrorism and put it in writing. President Luis Zapatero said this was "a victory for democracy, law and reason."

Chapter 11 – The Basque Country Today

The Northern Basque Country is physically located in France, and the Southern Basque Country is within the geographic borders of Spain. The term they use for their country is *Euskal Herria*, which simply means the "Basque Country" in their native tongue of *Euskara*.

The French Basque Country doesn't have its own individual administration. It is incorporated into France as the Pyrénées-Atlantique. The French Basques are currently calling for a separate administration and even use the term "Département du Pays Basque."

French Basque seashore

The Southern Basque Country consists of the Basque Autonomous Community and the Chartered Community of Navarre. By virtue of the Spanish Constitution of 1978, Navarre's populace didn't elect to become an autonomous community; instead, the people of Navarre still operate via the *fueros*, or charters of the past. The mainstream political party, the Navarrese People's Union, which is conservative, had preferred that arrangement, as they feared that many of the Leftists in Navarre would control too much power. For the justification of this move, the Navarrese relied upon what is called consuetudinary law, which is essentially a law that evolved through customary practice. A king was elected, along with a justice department. Most laws were based on older laws or customs.

Spanish Basque seashore

In Spain, the Statute of Basque Autonomy, also called the Statute of Gernika, was passed in 1979. It allows the provinces of Álava (Araba-Álava), Biscay, and Gipuzkoa to operate with their own government. It is similar to the states of America, though they are not subject to all federal laws. Each autonomous community has its own executive, legislative, and judicial system.

Basque Parliament and Government

The main body of the Basque Autonomous Community is located in the city of Vitoria-Gasteiz, just south of the city of Bilbao, in Álava, Spain. It is the umbrella of the local governing bodies.

The head administrator, called the *lehendakari*, is elected by the Basque Parliament. He is a member of a political party and has the most power in the Basque Autonomous Community. Instead of an individual head, a community might choose to have a coalition government composed of people representing various political parties.

The Basque Parliament consists of elective positions. The members legislate and monitor the actions and activities of the main government. Parliamentary duties include establishing and approving budgets. It is composed of seventy-five members, who serve for four years. Each territory has twenty-five representatives, regardless of population. These officials come from various political parties, but they must have a minimum of 5 percent of votes to qualify to run for office.

Departments are headed by appointed ministers. Below are some examples of the various departments.

Official Local Organization for the Historic Provinces

1. Provincial Administration

2. Juntas Generales ("General Councils")

There are fifty-one members of the Juntas Generales. They oversee a territory or district and are elected. They pass local regulations, including local budgets. They select the members of the Provincial Councils.

3. Provincial Councils

They are selected by the Juntas Generales. They appoint a team of deputies to perform various functions.

4. Town Councils

Council members are elective positions and are headed by a mayor. They provide transportation, fire department, sanitation, and the like. They charge local taxes for these services.

Public Resources and Administrative Departments

The Basque Country has all the services found in other countries. This includes:

Office of the President

Office of the Vice President

Department of Public Administration

Department of Finance

Department of Education

Department of Industry, Tourism, and Trade

Department of the Interior

Department of Housing and Social Affairs

Department of Culture

Department of Health

Department of Justice, Social Security, and Employment

Department of Transportation and Public Works

Department of the Environment

Department of Agriculture and Fishing

The current president of the Basque Country is Íñigo Urkullu. He hails from the Basque Nationalist Party. Ever since the protests and tragic terrorism felt as a result of ETA, the country has become very sensitive to political party matters. Currently, Andoni Ortuzar is the president of the Basque Nationalist Party. At the moment, the Nationalist Party is calling for more of a voice in issues within the Spanish Constitution that relate specifically to the Basque Country.

The president and vice president of the Basques have vital responsibilities in managing relations with the European Union. They also maintain close relations with Basques living abroad. The vice president's office also created the Basque Agency for Women. Their main focus is to ensure there are equal opportunities for women in Basque society. In fact, the Law on Equality between Men and Women was passed in 2005.

The Department of Finance and the Department of Public Administration oversee the budget and administer taxes, which includes public and foreign finances. The Department of Public Administration trains its personnel and all government employees working for public agencies.

The Department of Education guarantees free public education from infancy to the age of eighteen. School attendance is compulsory. Secondary education is also compulsory. Education beyond this is offered, which includes universities, polytechnic schools, and professional schools. Adult education courses are provided and feature the teaching of *Euskara* and Spanish.

The Department of Industry, Trade, and Tourism has web sites open to all Basques, including Basques living abroad. They have two important societies attached to it: the Association of Competitiveness, Science, and Technology, as well as the Basque Energy Board and the Society for the Promotion of Industry.

The Department of the Interior is responsible for traffic, the police department, and the police academy.

The Department of Housing provides government-sponsored housing for those in need, as well as providing related subsidies for them. This includes a division that helps with repairing and refurbishing living quarters. The Department of Social Affairs relates to the Office of Immigration. Laws regarding immigration are enforced and amended continually. Integration programs are presented to allow for easier assimilation into the Basque society. Immigration education services are also offered. This department provides programs for senior citizens, families, the disabled, drug addictions, and women.

The Department of Culture creates a calendar of public events open to all. Public theater, music, dance, and exhibitions are provided for the enjoyment and education of the public and tourists.

The Department of Health maintains the Basque hospitals, pharmacology centers, mental health facilities, and the like. It monitors drug prices for generic medications and provides information on the brands available.

The Department of Transportation and Public Works is in charge of railways, roads, airports, sanitation, seaports, and marinas.

The Department of the Environment manages land use and its impact on natural resources. Policies are in place that aid in the overall master plan for environmental protection. Future plans for land development go through this agency for approval and advice. Education programs are also offered.

The Department of Agriculture and Fishing deals with issues related to the use of lands for agriculture and fishing. An important factor is the proper protection of the environment and the avoidance of overexploitation of natural resources. Regulations for the proper raising of domestic wildlife are in place.

The Department of Justice, Social Security, and Employment oversees retirement benefits and unemployment. This includes job training if it is needed. It also provides for the training of public employees. There is an ancillary section that covers issues of job safety related to the workplace, accident prevention, and worker hygiene.

Local Practices

Humanitarian rights are enshrined in the local communities, especially the right not to be mistreated. Local responsibilities might be allocated by elections or even the drawing of lots to assume certain responsibilities.

The High Court of Justice

The court has thirteen members. Six are elected, and the other six are magistrates who have judicial powers pertinent to the offices they occupy. The last member is the president of the High Court of Justice. There are also presidents of the specific courts, namely the civil and criminal courts, the "contentious administration court," labor courts, and the magistrates of the provincial courts of Biscay, Álava, and Gipuzkoa.

The "contentious" court hears cases on appeals that deal with individual matters and the contended actions of administrators or administrations of governmental bodies. It is served by nine magistrates.

Labor courts hear cases related to the interests of employees, and they utilize tribunals to hear cases related to labor conflicts and bankruptcy. Ten magistrates serve in the labor courts.

Taxes

Tax agreements with Spain and the autonomous Basque regions are individually made. There are quotas that cover the provision of money for services provided by each Basque province that are not covered by Spain. For example, the individual provinces pay for road repairs, sanitation, local transportation, education, and the like. Spain provides the expenses for defense, foreign affairs, international representation, the running and maintenance of airports and seaports, and high-speed transportation for all its citizens, including the Basques.

Since 1981, the average quota for a Basque in an autonomous community is 6.24 percent of the national budget.

Each autonomous Basque community has its own personal income taxes, corporate taxes, inheritance taxes, and gift taxes. This money goes into the treasuries of the individual communities. Value-added taxes are charged by the communities on certain products, such as alcoholic beverages.

The Family Unit

Families in the Basque Country are composed much like the families of democratic cultures. Most consist of a heterosexual couple, who may or may not have children. This is true for about 44 percent of the population. There are also single parents living on their own, which represent about 20 percent of the population. Some live in family groups, like extended families.

Homosexuality isn't forbidden in Spain and the Basque Country. If a same-sex couple gets married in Spain, where it is recognized, the marriage is also recognized in the Basque Country.

As of 2003, domestic partnerships—two unmarried people living together—is rather common in the Basque Country. Unlike arrangements in other countries, these couples have the same rights and obligations as married couples. However, they do need to register as a couple in a domestic partnership. This even includes same-sex marriages, except in the case of the death of one of the partners. In that case, widower's pensions are not allowed. Regardless of sexual preference, all marriages permit adoptions, and they must pay taxes.

In 2005, the Gender Equality Act was passed. Emakunde is the institution attached to the office of the president that advises, coordinates, evaluates, and promotes gender equality for women. It works to ensure that gender equality is implemented in education, health, employment, culture, and social services.

Education

Education is provided free of charge. It is compulsory from ages six to sixteen. At the age of sixteen, students have the option to continue their education for two more years, provided they have satisfactory grades.

Students may then pursue academic studies through preparation training to enter college, or they can take professional courses to ready themselves for an occupation. Following the death of Francisco Franco, schools called *ikastolak* were created. Those schools are of four types: X, which teaches only in Spanish; A, which teaches in Spanish with Basque as a compulsory subject; B, which teaching is partly in Spanish and partly in Basque; and D, which education is taught only in Basque. It is interesting to note that 50 percent of the students elect to attend the all-Basque language schools.

There are four universities in the Basque Country: the public University of the Basque Country; the University of Deusto, a Jesuit-run university; the Opus Dei-run University of Navarre, a Catholic university; and the University of Mondragon, run by the Mondragon Corporation.

Business

Labor unions, called "class unions," aren't organized for each particular company. Instead, they represent all workers. Most are divided into geographical areas. ELA, which stands for *Eusko Langileen Alkartasuna* ("Basque Workers' Solidarity"), is nationalistic and supports the provinces in the Basque Country. CCOO is a huge labor union in Spain, and it oversees the Basque Country as well. CCOO stands for *Comisiones Obereras* ("Workers' Commissions"). There are also smaller unions representing different sectors of the country, such as education or health. Other unions represent the self-employed and farmers.

Many businesses are cooperatives, which are businesses that are run and owned by the workers. The Mondragon Corporation is an umbrella for 257 cooperative companies, which employ a little over 74,000 people. Not all of the workers live in the Basque Country. The beauty of the Mondragon Corporation is the fact that money is taken out of the general funds to rescue a member company that might be on the verge of bankruptcy.

The Basque business sector is virulent and above the general EU (European Union) average. Metalworks and steel are still their strongest industrial sectors, and they also make machine tools. Petrochemical products, aeronautics, and energy production are also strong.

Mondragon Corporation

The Mondragon Corporation is the largest cooperative corporation in the Basque Country. It was founded in 1941 by a priest named José María Arizmendiarrieta, and its original purpose was to help the Basques after the Spanish Civil War. The country had been devastated by poverty, and it was in sore need of educated labor. Arizmendiarrieta built a college that trained its students to be skilled technicians, engineers, and other trained laborers.

The Mondragon Corporation employs humanistic principles of understanding and mutual cooperation in improving its member companies. One of its pivotal principles is self-sufficiency. Their objective is to create companies that do not need to be too dependent upon other industries for survival. In some ways, it is the antithesis of the kind of competition that pits one company against another. Mondragon has a unique approach toward business, as it doesn't place the accumulation of wealth as its sole overriding precept. Factors like safety and quality feature high on their set of priorities. They are, of course, interested in profit but not to its extreme. Workers contribute to the cooperative to the extent of their abilities.

Mondragon holds up the rights of the workers and minimizes the exploitation of labor in favor of profit. In addition, it avoids heavily paying the few corporate executives on top so the benefits can be spread around to the other workers.

The Basque industrial area is in the north, and it progressively gets more agricultural as one heads south.

Culture

The Basques love festivals. The Festival of San Fermín, also known as the Running of the Bulls, is known worldwide. It goes on for a week, and it includes more than just the running of the bulls. Parades feature giant puppets dressed in what is known as "Basque Red," one of the colors in their flag.

It originated in the 13th century when bulls were shipped into Pamplona by barges in order to be brought to the market. Young men were assigned to run alongside the bulls to lead them through the streets and into their corrals to be auctioned off. After a while, they made a sport of it. Bullfights are also a popular pastime in both Spain and the Basque Country.

July and August are the most popular months for festivals and fairs. These celebrations are quite imaginative. For the Virgen Blanca celebration, a doll named Celedón, so-called after Juan Celedonio de Anzola from Vitoria-Gasteiz in the province of Álava, descends on a wire from the belfry at the Church of San Miguel to a balcony over New Square. He carries an umbrella, like the character Mary Poppins. Once the doll arrives, a real person, who is supposed to be the embodiment of Celedón, appears on the street. He gives a brief speech, which is followed by parades, cooking contests, bullfights, and fireworks.

Sports

The Basques have a series of rural sports and competitions, such as wood-chopping, hole drilling, scything, bale tossing, cob-carrying, stone lifting, and even tug-of-war. Animal-related competitions like ram fighting, sheep shearing, and donkey racing also take place.

The idi probak is a competition requiring an ox, horse, or donkey to drag heavy stones across a distance.

Their main sporting events are called pelota, which consists of a variety of handball-inspired court games.

Jai Alai

The sport of jai alai originated in the Basque Country in the 14th century. The Basque term for it is *zesta punta*, which literally means "basket tip." It is a variation of pelota. The sport has spread to Spain, France, North and South America, the Philippines, and Cuba. There are World Championship games held yearly. Jai alai is also one of the events in the Olympics.

Jai alai

The Tamborrada de San Sebastián Festival consists of parades and bands. It has a military flavor, as the drums are usually hand-crafted. They are based on designs from its original creator, an anonymous baker who started beating on barrels he was filling near San Vincente Church in 1720. The Basque people are very creative, and they find pleasure by making work seem less of a chore.

In the city of Bilboa, the people celebrate the Assumption of Our Lady in what is called Aste Nagusia, or "Great Week." Its central event is a circus, and there are traditional dancing performances. It originated during the dictatorship of Francisco Franco. Dancers, or *danzarias*, wear white with red berets when they perform for the people in Bayonne in the French Basque Country during their annual fair.

Basque danzarias

Another popular event is a non-competitive sponsored auto race through a complex course laid out in the foothills of the Pyrenees. Proceeds go to a general fund to teach and preserve *Euskara*, the unique language of the Basques.

Basque Cuisine

The cuisine of the Basques differs from one part of the country to the other. It shows a mixture of what the sea offers, as well as meat dishes featuring lamb and spices, such as Espelette pepper.

Fish, such as salted cod, tuna, and other seafood, dominate the coastal regions. A favorite dish is marmitako or "tuna pot." The Basques use albacore (longfin) tuna to create this meal. Kokotxa is a fish stew made from the cheeks of a fatty fish, like hake or cod. It is usually served with a white sauce that is made green due to its heavy parsley content. Elvers, or small eels, are also popular. Maja Squinado is a spiny crab with very long legs, and the Basques stuff and bake the crabs in their own shells. It is a common dish in the Bay of Biscay area. Txipirones, or small squids, are also quite common in those waters and can be eaten with their ink. Piperade is a soup made from an assortment of vegetables, mostly tomatoes. It is similar in taste to ratatouille. One more popular item is talo, which is a corn-like tortilla that can be used as a sandwich wrap. The Basques tend to use olive oil rather than vegetable oil in cooking since it is of a higher quality.

Many Basque people are genetically lactose-intolerant. However, many can tolerate sheep milk. Hence, they have cheese products such as Roncal or Ossau-Iraty, which is cheese made from ewe's milk. Idiazabal is a spreadable cheese made from sheep's milk. The lactose in this product is generally washed out when the whey is discarded.

The inland areas eat a lot of cured meats, such as ham and lamb sausage. Vegetables and legumes are plentiful in the fertile Ebro Valley. Txakoli is a popular light white or sparkling green wine that is low in alcoholic content and has a short shelf life. It originated in the Álava province, but there is a light rosé variety in Cantabria.

Apple cider is a popular alcoholic beverage in the Basque Country. Cider houses are called sidrerías in the Basque language. They also offer cod omelets and other light snacks. Red and rosé wines are produced in the Spanish vineyards of the province of Rioja. The city of Getaria in the Basque province of Gipuzkoa produces white wines.

The Basque Diaspora

Throughout the years, many Basques have left the Basque Country and settled in other parts of the world. Outside of France and Spain, the highest number of Basques have resettled in Columbia, Chile, and Argentina. There are also communities in Venezuela, Mexico, Peru, Cuba, Uruguay, Russia, other parts of Asia, Canada, the United States, and Saint Pierre and Miquelon. Saint Pierre and Miquelon is a group of French-owned islands in the northwestern Atlantic Ocean near Canada. The Basque communities have been there for many years and are mostly the descendants of Basque fishermen. The Basque flag is flown there, and it is the unofficial flag for these islands.

Conclusion

The history of the Basques is rather convoluted, as these proud people have been manipulated by much larger nations throughout the ages. Today, the Basques number about three million, and they have fought the good fight to preserve their language and culture from unjustifiable raids from others.

Throughout time, many civilizations who prized assimilation popped up, wanting to make the Basques more like them. Between 1892 and 1920, Francisco Franco, the dictator of Spain, forbade the Basques to speak their own native language. This was a common theme in history. Way back in 196 BCE, the ancient Romans tried to Romanize the Basques. Fortunately, neither Rome nor Franco was successful.

When the various territories of the Basque people were conquered by one foreign nation after another, no attention was paid to keeping their respective territories intact. Dividing up the Basque territories seemed to become an international game. What is more astonishing is the fact that these conquered territories were often renamed. Throughout the years, there was little effort spent on spelling the names of their people or their provinces in a consistent manner.

So, it is no wonder the Basque people of today have exerted a great deal of effort to preserve their language. In fact, long-term visitors have said they found it a valuable asset to learn *Euskara*, as they are awarded more respect for having done so.

It is amazing to note that these people, whose ancestry dates back to Paleolithic times, haven't lost much of the purity of their ethnicity. Researchers, ethnologists, and even medical clinicians have engaged in modern-day studies about these people. The Basques have been a subject of research all the way down to the level of their unique DNA.

The Basques are clever and intelligent. They have been practical since ancient times, having learned early on that one can earn money by being a mercenary in all the wars that peppered history. They also knew how to utilize their resources, and they were perhaps the most skilled whale hunters on the continent in the 15th century. It was the Basques who mined gold and silver for the Roman currency. The numismatists of today still sell Basque coins from ancient times.

The most prominent and laudable characteristic of the Basques is the fact that they work together. The comradery they have for each other is their greatest survival skill, and it has only grown throughout the centuries. Even their business community thrives on cooperation, rather than cut-throat competition. This is perhaps the key to their survival through the many wars fought around or even on their land.

Here's another book by Captivating History that you might like

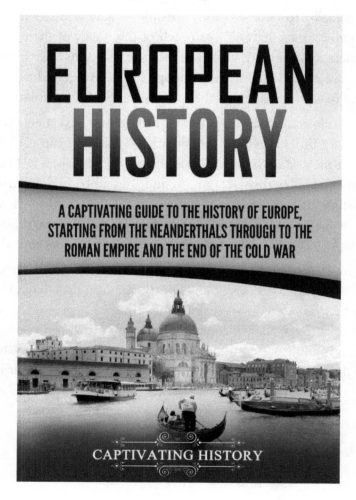

Free Bonus from Captivating History
(Available for a Limited time)

Hi History Lovers!

Now you have a chance to join our exclusive history list so you can get your first history ebook for free as well as discounts and a potential to get more history books for free! Simply visit the link below to join.

Captivatinghistory.com/ebook

Also, make sure to follow us on Facebook, Twitter and Youtube by searching for Captivating History.

Bibliography

"Ancient DNA Cracks Puzzle on Basque Origins" Retrieved from
https://www.bbc.com/news/science-environment-34175224

"Basque Country: A Land of Myths and Legends"
https://www.bizkaiatalent.eus/en/pais-vasco-te-espera/senas-de-identidad/vasco-tierra-leyendas/

"Basque Mythology, Ancestral Religion, Spirituality and Modern Religion" Retrieved from

https://aaconventionbiarritz.com/2019/08/29/basque-mythology-ancestral-religion-spirituality-and-modern-religions/

"The Basque Problem" Retrieved from
https://erenow.net/common/the-basque-history-of-the-world/3.php

"The Basque Paradigm" Maternal Evidence of a Maternal Continuity in the Franco-Cantabrian

Region since Neolithic Times" Retrieved from
https://www.ncbi.nlm.nih.gov/pmc/articles/PMC3309182/

"A Brief History of the Pamplona Citadel and City Walls" Retrieved from

https://theculturetrip.com/europe/spain/articles/a-brief-history-of-the-pamplona-citadel-and-city-walls/

Cabarello, D. "Parity in Government: Gender Equality within the Basque Government" Retrieved

from https://blogs.shu.edu/basqueresearch/2015/12/01/parity-in-parliament-gender-equality-within-the-basque-government/

Collins, Roger, Gillingham, J. (ed.) (1984) "The Basques in Aquitaine and Navarre: Problems of Frontier Government". *War and Society in the Middle Ages: Essays in Honor of J. O. Prestwich.*

Boydell Press

"History of Basque II" Retrieved from
http://www.kondaira.net/eng/Euskara2.html

"History of the Basque People" Retrieved from

https://thereaderwiki.com/en/History_of_the_Basque_people

"History of the Basque Wars" Retrieved from

http://forwhattheywereweare.blogspot.com/2011/10/history-of-basque-wars-i.html

"The History of Navarre" Retrieved from

http://www.bbc.co.uk/history/british/middle_ages/hundred_years_war_01.shtml

"The Hundred Years War" Retrieved from

http://www.bbc.co.uk/history/british/middle_ages/hundred_years_war_01.shtml

Watson, C. (2003) Modern Basque History: Eighteenth Century to the Present University of

Nevada, Center for Basque Studies

"We Are not our Ancestors: Evidence for Discontinuity between Prehistoric and Modern Europeans" Retrieved from
http://www.jogg.info/pages/22/Coffman.pdf

Printed in the USA
CPSIA information can be obtained
at www.ICGtesting.com
LVHW042312241123
764835LV00004B/81